EXPLORING CAREERS IN COMMUNICATIONS AND TELECOMMUNICATIONS

EXPLORING CAREERS IN COMMUNICATIONS AND TELECOMMUNICATIONS

By

John C. Zacharis

Frances Forde Plude

Andrew S. Rancer

THE ROSEN PUBLISHING GROUP, INC.

New York

Allen County Public Library
Ft. Wayne, Indiana

Published in 1985 by The Rosen Publishing Group, Inc.
29 East 21st Street, New York City, New York 10010

First Edition
Copyright 1985 by John C. Zacharis, Frances Forde Plude,
Andrew S. Rancer

Library of Congress Cataloging in Publication Data

Zacharis, John C.
  Exploring careers in communications and
telecommunications.

  1. Communication and traffic—Vocational guidance.
2. Telecommunication—Vocational guidance. 3. Mass
media—Vocational guidance. I. Plude, Frances Forde.
II. Rancer, Andrew S. III. Title.
HE152.5.Z33 1985   380.3′023   85–10814
ISBN 0–8239–0644–2

Manufactured in the United States of America

Cover design courtesy of Auxiliary Services, Miami-Dade
Community College, Miami, Florida

Dedicated to

Haig Der Marderosian (1931–1984)
A Great Teacher of Communication

John C. Zacharis   Frances Forde Plude   Andrew S. Rancer

About the Authors

The authors are members of the faculty and administration at Emerson College, Boston, Massachusetts. Founded in 1880, Emerson College is the only institution of higher education in the United States that is devoted exclusively to the study of the communications arts and sciences.

John C. Zacharis holds a B.S. and an M.S. from Emerson College and a Ph.D. from Indiana University. He is the Senior Vice President at Emerson and has served as Chairman of Communication Studies. He is the author of *Speech Communication: A Rational Approach*, with Coleman Bender, and *Your Future in the New World of Communications*. Dr. Zacharis has served as President of the Eastern Forensic Association and has held many other academic office. He has written speeches for many business leaders and politicians.

Frances Forde Plude holds a B.S. and an M.Ed. from Boston College, an M.A. from Emmanuel College, and an Ed.D. from Harvard University. She is President of Communications Technology Associates, a telecommunications consulting firm; she is Chairman of the

Board of Children's Television International in Washington, D.C.; she has served as a member of the Board of Directors of Instructional Television Associates in New York City and as development director of a ten-city ITFS broadcast network; and she was program director at WSBK-TV in Boston from 1961 to 1974. Dr. Plude currently chairs the Division of Mass Communication at Emerson College.

Andrew S. Rancer holds a B.A. and an M.A. from Queens College of C.U.N.Y. and a Ph.D. from Kent State University. Dr. Rancer is an Associate Professor of Communication Studies at Emerson College. He has written nationally syndicated articles on argumentativeness and has published many articles in such journals as the *Journal of Applied Communications Research*, the *Journal of Personality Measurement, Communication Quarterly*, and *Communication Education*. He has presented many papers at conventions, has served as communications consultant for several companies including American Express Company, and is editor of the *Massachusetts Speech Communication Journal*.

Acknowledgments

The authors are grateful to the many persons and organizations that provided information and assistance.

Kathy Sturges of the Career Services office at Emerson College provided materials, data, and resources. Many pictures were generously provided by the Public Relations office of the College, Bill Harrold, Director.

Data General Corporation, *Channels of Communications* magazine, and Miami-Dade Community College granted permission for the use of important graphics, pictures, and information.

Jane Cerrotti provided important assistance in the preparation of the manuscript.

President Allen E. Koenig of Emerson College offered his encouragement and the time to John Zacharis to commence this project.

Finally, the authors are very appreciative of their families' encouragement and support.

Contents

Preface

The fields of communications and telecommunications touch virtually every person, household, and industry in America. No one book can describe all the job opportunities to be found in the communications, information, and computer industries. So we have chosen to focus upon the traditional and newly developing communications and telecommunications careers in the electronic media, the print media, business communications including advertising and public relations, and education.

New technologies and products in video, satellites, cable, and computers will expand career possibilities in communications beyond their current rate of growth. *Exploring Careers in Communications and Telecommunications* looks at trends in these fields. Further, we look at job descriptions and the education required to get the jobs. Finally, we provide many resources, including books, organizations, and placement associations where you can find additional information about careers and specific job opportunities.

Is this a career direction you should take? This book should help you to evaluate your goals and answer that question.

Chapter I

Exploring Communications and Telecommunications

As the American economy continues to grow, so do new job opportunities. Nowhere has this been more obvious than in the fields of communications and telecommunications.

In 1880 nearly 50 percent of the work force in the United States was employed in agriculture and industry; only 5 percent in communications-related fields. By 1980 the communications and information industries employed 50 percent of the work force. That percentage is expected to increase to 70 percent by 1990.

What was once an industrial society, many authors have said, has changed to an information society. Communications, the production and storage of information, and the dissemination of knowledge are the things upon which the information society has been built.

What Are Communications and Telecommunications?

Communications and telecommunications are terms applied to systems by which information is sent from one place to another or from a sender to a receiver.

Language and human speech is one system of communication, but there are many others. Information may be sent by written symbols, visual messages, and dramatic forms. Each of us participates in the communication process as we converse in human language each day.

Information is sent, also, by electronic means such as television, radio, telephone, and computers. It may be coded into computer signals or sent by human language.

The terms *communications* and *telecommunications* are used by many industries to describe many different kinds of communication.

The Growth of Information Occupations
U.S. Work Force 1860-1980

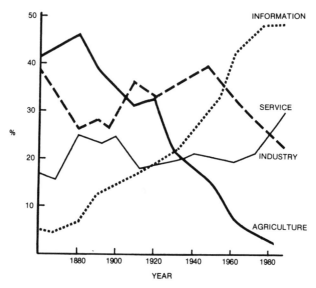

Source: Porat, *The Information Economy*, Vol. 1, P. 121

Telecommunications, which is derived from the Greek word *tele*, meaning *far*, usually refers to distant communication systems such as radio, television, cable, and satellite communications. But the term *communications* often refers to the same things. So we do not choose to make rigid distinctions between the terms. Career opportunities in communications may be found in fields that use both words.

Understanding Opportunities in Communications

To understand communications as a career, one must realize that there is a communications industry and other industries that use communications. Communications industries are those whose purpose it is to produce and sell communications. Examples are television, advertising, publishing, and motion pictures. Industries that *use* communications are many. Examples are agriculture and the steel and automobile industries. Each uses communications to organize or advertise the industry.

In the communications industry itself, job opportunities are increasing at a steady rate of 15 to 27 percent a year, according to the United States Bureau of Labor Statistics. This statistical average includes teaching, in which the growth rate is expected to be low (less than 5 percent) and other communications fields such as sales and marketing where the growth rate is as high as 50 percent. New opportunities are being created in many companies and organizations such as the following:

- 1,200 public relations firms
- 4,400 advertising agencies
- 1,000 television stations
- 9,000 radio stations
- 5,000 cable television systems
- 4,000 special-interest magazines
- 10,000 newspapers
- 22,000 magazines and newspapers combined

The United States Bureau of Industrial Economics has reported on the economic prospects for 200 national industries, including communications and telecommunications. Projected annual growth rates in the 1980's, based upon the value of sales, are as follows:

	Annual Growth Percentage (in sales)
Broadcasting	
Radio	12%
Television	13%
Cable	30%
Computing Equipment and Services	15%
Communications Electronic Equipment	10%
Telephone and Telegraph Services	7%
Printing and Publishing	3%

But facts alone can be misleading. Most job information about the communications industry refers to specific job titles such as announcer, broadcast technician, copywriter, and editor. Such job descriptions do not reflect the communications profession as a whole. People described as managers, for example, work in the field of communications either as writers, speakers, or salespersons. Many people are in communications who are not described as communications professionals. Real estate agents, for example, spend over 90 percent of their time in communications-related activities.

Thus it is important to look not only at the communications industry but at those industries that use communications. Of the top corporations in the United States, over 80 percent have communications departments that manage and produce media. There is a computer terminal for approximately every fifty jobholders in America. Doctors, lawyers, stockbrokers, air traffic controllers, teachers, and government officials all use computers as well as other forms of media and communications. The direct and indirect uses of communications and telecommunications are unlimited.

Communications and Telecommunications as a Career

Direction will be needed as you explore fields that are in a period of rapid growth, change, and development. The panorama of communications opportunities is wide and complex.

It is important to think first of a career path before you consider a specific job. There is a difference between a career and a job. A career in communications and telecommunications may encompass many types of jobs. A specific job, on the other hand, usually involves one job definition.

In considering a career, you need further to determine what type of *role* best fits your personality, preferences, and abilities. Do you like to perform, or are you better "behind the scenes"? Are you a technician, or are you creative? Do you prefer management, or do you enjoy analyzing problems?

The following role descriptions may help you to better define which communications role is suited to you.

You as a communicator. As a communicator, you are a direct participant in the communication process. You create the message or the act of communication. Newscasters are communicators. They gather, edit, and broadcast the news on television or radio. Likewise, the journalist writes for a magazine or a newspaper. The salesperson is a communicator. Television performers are communicators.

As a communicator, you will be required to think, to analyze, to interpret, and to present ideas. Success will depend upon self-confidence, a desire to place your particular stamp of originality on an idea, and talent. In this career it is important that you enjoy expressing yourself either in public or in writing.

You as a producer and manager of communications. The production of communications—whether it be an advertisement or a sales campaign—requires a producer or manager. In some fields, such as motion pictures, this person is called a producer. In advertising, this person may be called an account executive. In any case, this person designs, creates, manages, or directs communications. As a producer/manager, you might develop anything from a television program to a political campaign, to a small unit of programmed instruction, or to a videotape of a rock concert. You might design a computer system for a business or educational institution. You might manage an entire staff of public relations personnel.

Other producer/manager roles include audiovisual production, newspaper management, and the production of a sales medium: a trade or industrial show, a play, an opera, or a symphony. In short, this role requires that you produce whatever it takes to communicate an idea, whether it be entertainment or an information system. The producer/manager must also consider financial constraints. He or she must know about the materials and the technical skills to be used. Films might require the producer to employ cartoonists or animation experts. An industrial demonstration film would require the producer/manager to select or aid in the selection of actors and graphics personnel. The producer/manager must be involved from beginning to end in the development of a communications product. He may also be required to sell that product.

You as a communications analyst.   Because all communications and telecommunications are dependent upon systems, analysts serve as the designers, critics, and planners of systems. A communication system may be a highly complicated, integrated system involving computers, data banks, and cable television; or it may be a simple sales presentation.

Communications and telecommunications analysts determine how a system works best. They make recommendations for improvement. They recommend that certain parts of the system be changed, or that messages be communicated in different ways. In a field such as politics, the analyst might suggest how a candidate might better use television for effective advertising. He might suggest how a mail campaign might yield more votes.

Communications by mail has grown by staggering proportions in the last two decades. Products are sold through mail-order advertisements. Manufacturers determine those persons most likely to respond to a mail-order advertisement for a particular product. New homeowners, for example, may receive many advertisements about products related to the home. Retired persons receive mail advertisements about retirement communities.

The communications analyst might be involved in the creation of a mail-order campaign, the writing of the copy, the visual design of the brochure, and the selection of mailing lists. He or she might then *analyze* the effectiveness of the campaign. Did it return 3 percent in sales, or 5 percent? How can it be improved? What new mailing lists can be used? Each of these questions depends upon analysis and the determination of strategies for communication.

An analyst might also make suggestions as to how to improve human communications within a company. Because of conflicts within management, decisions may be delayed before being implemented. Or the company may be suffering from problems related to its public image. The analyst will determine what strategies can improve the overall human communication systems within the company.

You as a communications and telecommunications technologist. Many people like to consider themselves as doers or hands-on practitioners. Technologists are involved in the manufacturing, operation, and maintenance of communications systems and equipment. In artistic forms of communications, the technologist may be involved in commercial art, photography, filming, television operations, layout design, or lighting. In electronic communications, the technologist may be involved in replacement and maintenance of equipment, engineering, and programming.

Interrelating your roles. These descriptions of communications roles are useful only in understanding the type of work that you might prefer. Your preference, however, may not involve only one role. Many careers in communications require the interrelation of roles. A good producer/manager may also need to be an effective analyst. A good communicator may also need to be a knowledgeable technician.

As an example of how various roles are interrelated and how roles relate to specific jobs, an imaginary job chart is given below. In the left column are listed all of the jobs that go into the inventing, manufacturing, and selling of an imaginary product. The communications skills and roles required to do those jobs are listed in the center and at the right. Note the various combinations of skills and roles that take place as the product goes through its various stages.

Product	Communications Skill	Role
The product idea	Understanding of the needs of people for the product	Communications analyst
Presenting the product to the board of directors	Knowing the company's best interests	Communications analyst
	Writing and delivering the presentation	Communicator

Product	Communications Skill	Role
	Developing aids (such as slides, models) for the presentation	Communications producer-technologist
Decision to produce the product	Analyzing the information	Communications analyst
	Conference techniques; making a decision	Communicator
Production	Designing features that appeal to people	Communications producer-analyst
	Instructions to employees on how to make the product	Communications producer; also communicator
	Establishing steps in the communications process during production	Communications analyst
Marketing and advertising	Determining the market; understanding the public: what people will buy the product?	Communications analyst
	Developing ways in which to market the product	Communications analyst-producer
	Developing advertisements	Communications producer
	Performing in advertisements	Communicator
	Making the advertisement	Communications technologist
Selling the product	Developing a sales approach	Communications analyst-producer
	Developing a sales kit	Communications producer
	Developing an order and supply system	Communications analyst
	Direct selling	Communicator

Defining your role. The roles described above should not be confused with actual job descriptions. A search of the classified advertisements is not likely to yield jobs such as "communicator," "communications producer," "communications analyst," or "communications technologist." This is simply a way of defining your career goals in an extremely broad field.

The following chapters list many specific job titles available in all the related fields of communications. An interesting exercise that may reveal a lot about yourself is to list some of the job descriptions from this book that really appeal to you. To the right of each job description, list the communications role of the job. Use the roles we have just discussed: communicator, communications producer, communications analyst, and communications technologist.

An example of the exercise is as follows:

Jobs That Interest You	*Communications Role*
Television announcer	Communicator
News reporter	Communicator
Public-relations writer	Communicator

From this simple exercise, you will see how often you have picked jobs that have the same type of role. You should then be able to make a clearer decision about your career direction. Having designated your communications role, you will then be able to prepare accordingly.

Evaluating Yourself for a Communications/ Telecommunications Career

You have seen the various communication roles. You have looked at the jobs in the basic communications professions. Now, you must evaluate yourself—honestly. Is your interest real? Are you prepared to take the educational steps? Are you suited for a communications career?

Making positive career decisions is dependent upon a process of examining yourself and the world of work. This book focuses mostly upon the world of work in communications, its opportunities and careers. You, however, must assess yourself by looking into your past and present so as to identify personal qualities, interests, skills, abilities, and values. By understanding who you are, you will be able to look into your future to establish some goals.

Evaluating Your Interest

If you have reached the point of reading a book about communications careers—namely, this book—the chances are that your interest is not a passing one. On the other hand, communications is a field that attracts many by its glamour alone. A popular television personality, a favorite writer, or an exciting speaker may have turned you on *for the moment.* Be careful. The communications profession is, like all fields, hard work.

You might begin by asking yourself how you first became interested. What stimulated you? Was it the result of a casual conversation with a friend, a magazine article, or a late-night talk show? If so, you need more exploration. But if the thought of a communications career came out of a realization about yourself and your natural interests, then it is probable that you have discovered a future you can stay with.

The first key to evaluating your interest is *involvement*, or participation. If you like working with words, in writing or in speaking, then your interest is real. If your interest in words stops at the listening or reading stage, then you need to question yourself a bit more.

If you like to draw, paint, or construct creative objects, then your interest is real. If, on the other hand, you merely enjoy attractive objects, then your interest is incomplete. It may be there, but it needs development.

Also, if you like photography, filming, or tinkering with communication equipment, then your interest is solid. But if your interest in communications ends soon after you have turned off the car radio, then you ought to wonder just how far it will take you.

Because you are entertained by communications does not mean that you will enjoy working in the field. Involvement is essential, even if you can see it only in your desire to write letters, in your impulse to speak up in class (or in public), or in your initiative to sell things for a worthy cause or for profit. A *habit* of communication should already be within you, or you must develop it. Otherwise, your interest may simply be on the surface. A deep-rooted attitude of wanting to do it must first captivate you.

A second way of evaluating your interest is to think of the values upon which it is built. Are these values, or attitudes, ones that will keep your interest over the years? Are they strong enough to take you through the difficult times? Consider your interest in communications from these five values—or points of view:

Professional excitement. We have talked about communications in several professions—from teaching to selling, from writing to producing, and from speaking to marketing. A basic function of each is communications. It encompasses an understanding of the times in which we live—a "with it" attitude. A knowledge of human behavior acquired from reading and experience and a capacity for using all types of communications are necessary. Is this something that can be of permanent value in *your* life? Do its possibilities generate professional excitement in you? Do you want to acquire the sharpness, quickness, and polish of the professional? Will you accept the challenge of perfection? You must—because it can be obtained only from drill and repetition.

Personal challenge. Much of your satisfaction in a career will come from the outside—the rewards you receive and the people you meet. But the real test of satisfaction will have to come from within. We have spoken about the advertising profession, which, according to many executives, gains its popularity from the satisfaction of creativity. The same is true throughout all communications fields. You can set high standards for yourself and then see the accomplished product of your thought and effort. Once you get your creative energy going, you will find that nothing seems too difficult. You will want to take on all challenges. In an age when people settle for ordinary lives and careers, this is an enviable position. To be sure, communications is not humdrum.

Financial reward. The measurement of success in communications cannot be set at a specific price, or predictable salary scale. The range is enormous. In the media or films, the rewards can be extraordinary—higher than most professions in the nation. But the risks are equally high. In the more secure writing or teaching positions, the rewards are modest. But the ability to communicate is always marketable, and a better-than-average talent will secure for you a permanent and solid career. Most important is the fact that your talents are hardly of the assembly-line variety. There is little chance for boredom. Speech-writing abilities, for example, can take you from working in politics to government, to business, to law—in a single year!

Fulfilling your self-image. Communicators are not meek or defeatist people. The extroverts and optimists seem to succeed.

High goals and a high sense of personal standards provide the fuel necessary to set you on your way to success. But it is important to know the difference between your real self and your ideal self. To confuse what you *think* you can do with what you *actually* can do may distort your sense of reality. You will need to know what steps to take to move from one level of accomplishment to the next. In each step, you will find rewards and an increasing sense of self-confidence. However, you should not fool yourself by attempting a giant step before learning the basics. Communications is an art, and one must learn the "parts" before attempting the "whole." In that way, your self-image will be fulfilled.

Judging your commitment by time. Success in communications depends largely on the strength of your commitment, and there is no better way to judge your commitment than by time. A short-term interest is not trustworthy. Only a compelling interest—one that you cannot put out of your mind—is worth following. A commitment that is the product of fantasy or daydreams is likely to collapse at the first roadblock.

Evaluating Your Personality

It is impossible to get a totally accurate picture of your personality. Nor is it possible to say that one personality type is better suited for communications than another. The roles and tasks are too diverse and unpredictable. However, you can try to see whether you have the personality *traits* that are commonly found in the field of communications. Several basic and very general categories are set forth below with the hope that you can obtain an estimate of yourself. A communications worker is . . .

A creator. Nothing is more important to communications than creativity. Even if your job is technical (you are a television camera-man, for example), a spark of creativity and imagination should always be with you. Your mind ought to be capable of thinking of interesting words and images. More than any other career, communications relies on people whose thinking is always fresh and exciting. The public craves newness and variety, and the good communicator has to be prepared to provide them. Do you have a good sense of color? Can you take photographs from original and interesting angles? Can you make a clean and attractive poster? Can you read a line of poetry, drama, or prose in a captivating way? Can you tell breathtaking stories? These are questions that you ought to answer positively.

An appreciator. Even if you are not yet a creator, you should have an appreciative interest in music, art, and literature. Appreciation of things creative shows a high degree of sensitivity and emotional energy. It is a quality that enables you to distinguish between what is good and bad, imaginative and trite, and new and old. Appreciation involves the process of *balancing one's senses* so as to see, read, or hear as much as possible from one work.

An appetite for good art or music provides nourishment to the creator. Having sensed something good in one work, the creator can rework it into his own. Having sensed something bad, he can discard it. Appreciation is needed for growth and development.

A leader. A corporate president or politician is a leader, and they have used communications effectively to succeed. But in the profession of communications, leadership refers more to the quality of being "out front." It means that you should be the type of person who starts ideas and who can get people's support for those ideas. You should not want to shy away from the limelight, whether it be in speaking, announcing, sales, or public relations. In education, the quality of leadership shows up in the person who enjoys teaching. The effective teacher can stand before a group of students and motivate them to think, do, and act.

But leadership does not mean egoism, dictatorship, or a desire to boss people. Leadership is more of a self quality than a quality of being able to lead groups. In communications, there are very few clear-cut "leaders" and "followers." There is much give and take. The leader is one who, by his stick-to-it attitude and creativity, can make his ideas attractive to those around him. He is the person with charisma and magnetism.

This brand of leadership is common in communications. Because the field has many uncertainties, much creativity, and a lot of guesswork about human behavior, you cannot sit back and expect your ideas to sell automatically to those around you. What is good is not always obvious. You will have competitors—also with good ideas. You must be ready to use all of your talents to generate interest in the worth of your point of view. In short, you must stay "on top" of the job.

Organizer.   A quality that is complementary to leadership is a sense of organization. "Organization" is not meant to suggest the military variety, which is abrupt, quick, and inflexible. Many situations will arise in communications that seem to defy the very possibility of organization. The creative man usually gets his ideas spontaneously and in disorganized ways. A teacher might interrupt his organization of notes or lesson plan in order to move into something new and exciting.

Yet organization is necessary. It is seen in successful people who are flexible yet persistent. This type of organization combines the qualities of the artist—which are often confusing—with all the qualities of leadership—which get things done. The best organizer in communications is simply the person who can set firm deadlines and clear goals. But the way in which he arrives at those goals may not always have the appearance of organization. Creativity simply does not work that way.

An enjoyer of people.   For communications to take place, people must obviously communicate with one another. Thus, the communicator must find enjoyment in people. As a communicator, you must be sensitive to their needs, you must be aware of their habits and cultural backgrounds, and you must know their temperaments and tastes. You must know what makes people different. A natural and honest sense of goodwill toward others will reflect in what you do. Likewise, a sense or feeling about people will provide insights that are essential for the creation of marketing campaigns, advertisements, or whatever.

A thinker.   A person in communications should not consider his work a nine-to-five occupation. He must be alert, constantly, for new ideas. Stimulating thoughts can come at any time, anywhere. A billboard, a sign, a certain combination of colors, a sermon, a short poem—anything may set you off. You should be willing to think about it—not quickly, but thoroughly. The best communicators are always observant.

Although communications will be the main job of your profession, up to 75 percent of your time will be spent in thought and in listening to others. You should train your mind, therefore, to jot down new ideas constantly. One psychologist maintains that the most thoughtful and creative period of the day is just before you fall asleep. Don't ignore such quiet moments to reflect and consider ideas.

A city dweller. Wherever there are the largest groups of people, you will find the greatest need for communications. All institutions seem to depend heavily upon the city as a source of ideas, a marketplace for products, a place of contact with mass media, and a center for art, music, and conferences. Advertising and public-relations firms function well in cities.

You should, therefore, enjoy cities. If you prefer the country, the chances are that the independently creative communication professions such as free-lance writing and art will be those in which you will be most comfortable. But the city provides the forum of give and take for contemporary ideas. Art exhibits, new music, and experimental drama will stimulate new thoughts. Most significant is the fact that most opportunities in communications are to be found in the city.

A pragmatist. Most dictionaries define pragmatist as a "practical business-minded individual." Such a description seems to conflict with the creativity expected of the communications profession. But creativity is used to accomplish some very practical objectives, one of which is to communicate to the greatest number of people. This is an objective that demands simplicity and directness. The pure artist might find this approach too "compromising" or commercial.

The communications professional, however, is one who can adjust himself to the pragmatic side. What he produces cannot be produced in a vacuum. It must be done with public tastes in mind. Once you have achieved stature and reputation in the field, you will be given greater freedom of expression.

A broad-minded person. If you have the personality traits just described, you probably are broad-minded. It should be particularly apparent in your open-mindedness toward people who may be radically different from you in attitudes and life-styles. In other words, you will have to adjust to people and situations quite different from those you are used to.

A traveler. Communications people are always on the go. They have to meet deadlines, meet people, observe situations firsthand, report news or ideas, and present ideas to many people in many places. If you dislike travel, you may also dislike some careers in communications. Remember that communications is global. Information moves from one source to another at incomprehensible speeds. The process of collecting, digesting, reporting, and putting such information into new styles may require you to adapt to geographical, as well as personality, changes.

Apart from professional assignments that may take you to various parts of the world, travel has much educational value as well. It allows you to rest and reflect, yet it also stimulates your mind. In order to stay creative, you will need to expose yourself to new places and situations. A comfortable and predictable routine leads to a dulling of the senses. So, consider travel. It's important.

Ten personality traits have been set forth. If you match up, it is *likely* (not guaranteed) that you have the qualities for a successful, rewarding, and stimulating career in communications. As a quick test, rank yourself according to the following scale:

> 1   lowest rating
> 2   low rating
> 3   average rating
> 4   high rating
> 5   highest rating

Rank yourself by placing an "X" in the appropriate box.

PERSONALITY TRAIT	1	2	3	4	5
Creativity					
Appreciation					
Leadership					
Organization					
Enjoyment of People					
Thinking					
Enjoyment of Cities					
Pragmatism					
Broad-mindedness					
Enjoyment of Travel					

Total Your Score._____

Ask four other persons to rank you with the same test. Ask a parent, a teacher, a friend, and someone who knows you, but not closely. For an accurate picture, see how their rankings match with yours. If your score averages less than 30 points, you should give more thought to communications before you enter it as a career.

Evaluating Your Academic Background

Glance back upon your education and ask the same kinds of questions that you asked of your personality. Which courses brought out your creativity, appreciation, leadership? Which teachers got you to think, organize, and work with people? Did you learn something about pragmatism and broad-mindedness? Did you enjoy studying about cities and distant places?

Many of these answers can be found in an appraisal of how you have done, or are doing, in courses. It ought to say a lot about what interests you have established for yourself. Even in those subjects in which you may have done poorly, you should have made some improvement in the areas most basic to communications:

1. Writing and speaking
2. Social understanding
3. Creative ability
4. Computer studies

You may also examine your experiences and functional skills. The following list of functional skills may tell you whether or not you would enjoy a career in communications. Which do you prefer?

Functional Skills

Persuading others
Instructing/teaching
Solving problems
Monitoring others' progress
Collecting information
Interviewing people
Negotiating with people
Coaching for performance
Announcing
Acting
Public speaking
Meeting the public
Speech-writing
Creative writing

Radio production
Technical drafting
Film production
Inventing new ideas
Managing other people
Orderly record-keeping
Providing a personal service
Supervising others' work
Researching in the field
Making monetary decisions
Creating
Directing performances
Editing written work
Feature writing

Language usage
TV production
Dramatic presentation
Working under pressure
Listening
Eye-hand-body coordination
Meeting deadlines
Overcoming obstacles
Motivating others
Preparing written documents
Library research
Planning programs
Coordinating events
Training others
Operating technical equipment
Writing for popular audience
Playing musical instrument
Critical writing
Physical exertion
Dance
Dependability
Reporting
Synthesizing numerical data
Achieving goals
Analyzing quantitative data
Business correspondence
Organizing data
Organizing people
Selling ideas
Arranging social events
Selecting
Thinking ahead
Investigating and studying
Appreciation of nature
Self-organizing
Rehearsing/practicing

Self-discipline
Photography
Design of interiors
Creating visual displays
Mechanical work
Electrical work
Work with visual media
Creating with your hands
Writing instructions for others
Selling with words
Counseling others
Vocal tasks
Fund raising
Organizing leisure time for others
Promotional work
Performing
Oral interpretation
Helping others with physical problems
Committee work
Laboratory work
Confronting others
Legal activity/advice
Entertainment
Keeping track of funds
Drawing diagrams, charts
Engineering design work
Stage construction or building
Computing quantifiable data
Managing information
Makeup work
Summarizing
Inspecting
Delegating
Appreciation of beauty
Administrative tasks
Evaluating

Evaluating Yourself Through Standardized Tests

The above list can provide a simple estimate of your interests and abilities. There are, however, more precise ways of evaluating yourself in the form of standardized tests.

Although tests can sometimes be misleading, they do offer the opportunity to see yourself as compared with others. If one test does not provide a satisfactory appraisal of yourself, try another. Some sort of clear pattern of information about your personality, vocational abilities, aptitudes, and skills is bound to emerge after several tests. There are several advantages to taking such tests:

1. They may detect unknown vocational interests and aptitudes that you could put to use.
2. They may confirm or deny your career goals. If they confirm them, you may proceed with more confidence. If they deny them, you have the chance to look into your abilities a little further.
3. They compare you to many thousands of other students.
4. They do not pass judgment. You need not fear "passing" or "failing." They simply provide you with information about yourself.

More than likely, you have already taken such tests. But if you have not, ask your guidance counselor, principal, or dean about obtaining one or several. The investment of time is well worth it.

You have just looked at the broad field of communications and telecommunications. You have examined your interests and considered which roles may be appealing to you. Now it is time to look at trends in communications and job descriptions in order to determine your career choices.

Chapter **II**

A World Wired for Telecommunications

Meet Liz Young

> *Dr. Elizabeth Young until recently worked as President of the Public Service Satellite Consortium. Liz Young's career shows how jobs are changing in our new world of telecommunications. A few years ago, in Ohio, she directed a statewide system of educational television stations. While employed in Washington, she worked connecting colleges in America with a communications satellite network. Now she's a vice president of a large satellite company.*

From television to satellites—that's where the world seems to be heading. All these changes mean career shifts in the years ahead. Like Liz, you will shift gears often as you move through your work life. One of the biggest career challenges today is learning to grow and to *re*train as new communications technologies alter the workplace. Here are some interesting trends to look for as you do your career planning:

- Many more *options* or *choices* arise as communications technologies multiply and change.
  Result: Today and in the future it will be necessary to *re*train regularly just to keep up with new technology thrusts and resulting job changes.

- Communication *links* mean that the location of the workplace is more flexible.
  Result: Some people can work at home, and people can meet regularly in teleconferences, connected by computer, audio, or video links.

- Some jobs will disappear, but others will emerge.
  Result: With computer data banks we can monitor job needs

better, so we should be able to be well prepared for changes. In addition, we can use new technology tools to train people for emerging job fields (such as video cassette and videodisc training courses).

- In many communications technology areas, more job-*sharing* will enable people to work fewer hours and time-share jobs.
Result: During leisure time people will tend to use more communications tools for entertainment and for instruction. This trend will allow both women and men to work at home part of the time, and it will have an impact on family life-styles.

The Information/Communication Society

A recent study showed that the United States has reached a point at which the major product we manufacture is *information.* About half of all workers are engaged in the handling of or communicating of information.

The following categories of workers all produce information, or store it, or communicate it:

- Computer service technician
- Computer systems analyst-programmer/operator
- Electrical or electronic technician

Other information industries include:

- Telephone
- Postal Service
- Radio, television, and communications fields
- Motion pictures
- Advertising
- Libraries and schools
- Banking and credit

The age of information requires an extensive network of avenues of communication—electronic roadways over which the information travels. This network is similar to major roads such as interstate highways branching to smaller roadways. The communications highways of the information age are interconnected in a vast pattern that includes television and radio transmitters, communication satellites, computer networks, data banks where information is stored, telephones and their vast interconnected links, and much more.

A business operation that clearly reflects the American specialization in the information product.

Each part of this information-transfer highway system has job slots—workers who organize the communication/information and keep it traveling over the various transmission routes. Those workers include:

Computer software writers
Graphic layout artists for computers
Cable television personnel
Advertising workers for new types of communications outlets
Telemarketing staff for retail sales via video screens
Editors and directors for teletext material
Laser technicians

Communications workers in the information society will have to deal with still other realities that are changing the work environment. The following are some job- and career-related factors:

- Each year, nearly 4 percent of all workers will be in some kind of job-training program.
- A serious shortage will exist in engineering areas, especially computer software specialists.
- A geographic shift is occurring, with workers moving to the Southwest. The largest population growth will occur in California, Florida, and Texas.
- Among companies there is a growing decentralization of operations; workers are less inclined to move from one location to another than they used to be.
- Information travels faster over the communications highways, so sender and receiver are brought closer together. The quantity of information increases also, since we can respond faster and more often.
- Computer technology can replace workers just as mechanization did in the industrial age.
- By the year 2000 the workweek will probably have dropped from 40 hours per week to 25 hours, with many employees sharing jobs.
- Unions will redirect their priorities to deal with decreasing job openings, increased retraining needs, and increasing numbers of working women.
- Service jobs will increase.
- Increasing numbers of people will be self-employed or work in small-business settings.
- Families are changing, with many new patterns emerging: single parents; two-career couples; a female breadwinner and a househusband.
- Microprocessors will mean that production and service jobs will require less skill, but engineers and supervisors will need increased skills and training.

The Fast Pace of New Opportunities

So what lies ahead for each of us seeking a career in our age of information? We will have increasingly exciting new options as technology opens doors to new opportunities. There may well emerge a work culture with highly paid, creative jobs for the information elite and many low-paid workers—with no large group in the middle.

One dramatic aspect of this revolution is its *pace*. The writer Frederick Williams notes that in the last eighty years more new forms of communications have developed than in all the previous 360 centuries. If those 360 centuries were reduced to a twenty-four-hour day, most communications technologies would have appeared in the last few minutes:

- At 8:00 p.m. the written word emerges (4000 B.C.)
- At 11:30 p.m. the Gutenberg Bible is printed
- At 11:56:48 p.m. commercial radio appears
- At 11:58:02 p.m. color television appears

And in the last two minutes of our twenty-four-hour day appear satellites, computer time-sharing, the portable TV camera, home TV recording equipment, and computer memory advances!

The Impact of New Technologies

Meet Herb Granath

Herb Granath attended Fordham University as a young man; he has spent twenty-five years in broadcasting. He has worked in radio and TV at NBC and ABC, and he has had a lot of experience in broadcast sales and program production. In the late 1970s Herb became responsible for new technologies at ABC Video Enterprises. He's a good example of a person whose communications career has moved him away from radio/TV as we've known it; now he studies and serves many new video technology markets.

In a recent interview, Herb Granath explained that ABC is producing a lot of video programming for people who own videocassette recorders (VCRs), as well as videodisc users. The network packages special tapes of events such as the American visit of Pope John Paul II and the Olympics, as well as many "how-to" tapes. Other new ABC developments:

- Touch-of-Home is a videocassette service for Americans living abroad.
- Video programs have been developed that feature theatrical productions.
- ABC News materials can be marketed in ten-minute modules for classroom use.
- Made-for-TV movies and other productions can have many different kinds of distribution, including ABC-affiliated stations, cable systems, pay-TV operations, and the international market.

Other ideas include a women's programming service distributed to cable systems by satellite; and a service that allows the network to deliver specialized shows (such as medical programs) between 1 a.m. and 6 a.m., "dumping" the program material by satellite through a system of specially activated videocassette recorders.

Granath and ABC Video Enterprises are moving to supplement wide *broad*cast services with new *narrow*casting video. All networks and major broadcast outlets are exploring these new avenues.

Figure 1 details the variety of new communications technologies. To plan for careers in these fields it will be helpful to see the overall relationship, the *pattern* of technologies. Once you see the picture as a whole, you can focus on individual areas and learn more specific details about its impact on career planning.

The new technologies fall into three categories: delivery systems, two-way technologies, and storage/programming technologies.

The most familiar category is that of regular channels for communications delivery, such as radio, TV, and cable. However, a lot of new activity is occurring in the second category, interactive communications fields. The most familiar interactive model is the telephone, a two-way device that we use all the time. The silicon chip and computer technology have made many other interactive options available, such as video games and machine banking and shopping.

The third area, the development and storage of program materials for new technologies, is the development of software for telecommunications.

Of course, many of these categories overlap in the job world. Companies or organizations are involved in several categories simultaneously. The computer, the major new-technology tool, is at the heart of almost all the technologies listed. Chips and computers are especially significant in interactive technologies and in the storage and analysis of data and instruction.

With all these changes occurring, career planning is both complicated and exciting.

Communications Delivery Systems	Interactive (Two-way) Technologies	Storage Technologies
	THE COMPUTER	
a. Broadcasting: Nonprofit (public) and commercial radio/TV stations (including stereo broadcasting)	a. Telephones (including cellular/mobile phones)	PROGRAMS
		a. Films
	b. Automated banking/ shopping	b. Video
	c. Videotext	c. Computer programs
b. Cable TV		
c. Satellites	d. Video games	d. Training materials

Communications Delivery Systems	Interactive (Two-way) Technologies	Storage Technologies
d. Videocassette recorders	e. Videodisc	
e. Pay television (STV, MMDS, SMATV, pay TV services, and pay-per-view)	f. Home security system	
	g. Teleconferences	
	h. Electronic mail	

Fig. 1. New Technologies

Communications Delivery Systems

"Broadcast" communications means the sending of an audio or video signal one way from one point to many points. By 1982 this was a $12 billion dollar business.

Network television represents one of the most powerful broadcasting communications systems ever developed.

Figure 2 details the number of broadcast radio and TV stations in the United States. Among these broadcasters are nonprofit and commercial stations. Some nonprofit stations are installed at colleges, where students can get early experience.

```
AM Radio .................... 4848
FM Radio.................... 3779
FM Educational Radio ......... 1244
UHF Commercial TV ........... 463
VHF Commercial TV ........... 535
UHF Educational TV ........... 187
VHF Educational TV ........... 116
```

Source: FCC

Fig. 2. Broadcasting Stations

Radio stations and listeners continue to increase, and network television still attracts major audiences. And now broadcasters themselves are investing in new communications technologies.

Cable television growth is shown in Figure 3 as moving rapidly to surpass 40 percent of American homes. (More than 5,700 cable systems serve over 33 million American homes.) The largest cable companies, as shown in Figure 4, will lead in developing new job opportunities. Cable offers many delivery channels in the newer systems, so that a variety of programs can be sent: movies, cable radio, special community/arts events, sports, computer data, and teleshopping. A cable system can serve as a municipal communications system by linking schools, libraries, police, hospitals, and fire departments, almost as in a telephone system.

Cable operations are widely varied. Some are national, such as Ted Turner's Cable News Network in Atlanta. In contrast, many local cable companies are small. But career opportunities do exist as cities and towns begin to use cable as an effective delivery system. As advertising on cable grows, so will sales opportunities. Many women find cable a good opportunity for advancement, since media sales is often a good route to management positions in communications companies.

Cable growth occurred mainly because of another technology: communications satellites. Many people believe that the first satellite, launched over a decade ago, was like the Golden Spike that in 1869

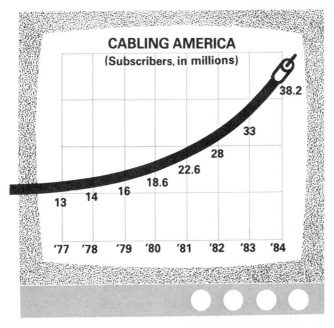

Fig. 3.

CABLE'S TOP TEN

	No. of Subscribers	No. of Franchises
1. TeleCommunications (TCI)	2,297,000	428
2. Time Inc. (ATC)	2,267,000	119
3. Group W Cable	1,872,000	140
4. Cox Cable	1,379,000	58
5. Warner Amex	1,340,000	146
6. Storer Communications	1,291,000	122
7. Times Mirror	858,000	67
8. Rogers/UA Columbia	776,000	22
9. Newhouse	742,000	64
10. Continental	686,000	66

Source: Cable TV Investor Newsletter

COURTESY CHANNELS OF COMMUNICATION

Fig. 4.

completed the transcontinental railroad. Located 22,300 miles out in space, the satellite receives signals from the earth and distributes them to a large part of the United States as if it were a tall television tower. Satellites transmit telephone calls, computer data, and video, including movies from pay-TV services such as Home Box Office (HBO). Cable companies receive programming from satellites and feed it into homes. If the direct broadcast satellite (DBS) becomes a reality soon, more sophisticated satellites will beam programs directly to small receiving dishes on the rooftops of homes. This will be especially welcomed by the millions of rural Americans who are unable to receive broadcasts

THE VCR COMES HOME

Average selling prices drop, more people own VCRs,
and more prerecorded tapes become available.

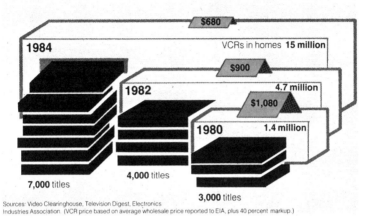

Sources: Video Clearinghouse, Television Digest, Electronics
Industries Association. (VCR price based on average wholesale price reported to EIA, plus 40 percent markup.)

COURTESY CHANNELS OF COMMUNICATION

Fig. 5

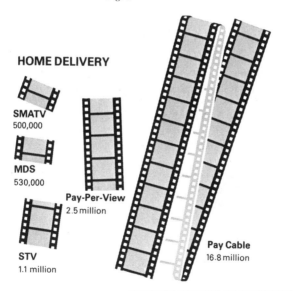

COURTESY CHANNELS OF COMMUNICATION

Fig. 6.

now because of their remote location. Like the computer, the communications satellite is a vital *link*.

Another fast-growing communications delivery system is the videocassette recorder, or VCR. Recent years have seen an astounding growth in VCR sales, as shown in Figure 5, and many small shopping centers have stores that rent cassettes (and recorders) overnight or for a weekend. Some recorders can be programmed so that the machine will turn itself on and off many times (when you are away and wish to record a program). Or you can watch one show and record another channel simultaneously. Stereo sound recording is also available in some of the higher-priced units.

A variety of other video program delivery systems exist. See Figure 6 for a comparison of audience size.

Pay-TV is a delivery system under which viewers pay by the month or by the show for the special service. Subscription television (STV) is transmitted over the air by a local TV station but is limited to one channel. SMATV is a master-antenna service used mainly by apartment or condominium dwellers. Multipoint distribution service (MDS) uses microwave technology for its transmission; it can offer multiple channels (eight, for example), thus making it a major competitor to cable systems.

Impact on Careers of Delivery Systems

In reviewing new communications delivery systems, some career trends can be noted:

- The telecommunications delivery marketplace has been broken up into many pieces. This means that smaller media markets will emerge, with job opportunities more focused on special areas.
- Advertising dollars will be spent in many of these varied areas, opening up sales opportunities (on a smaller scale, in some cases). Many individuals can gain experience in these smaller areas and later move up to larger markets.
- Many pay delivery systems depend on encoding systems, technologies that allow program delivery to special "addresses" only. This is one example of related or subordinated job opportunity areas.
- As communications delivery systems become more familiar, with VCRs moving into our homes and cable systems moving into our communities, more people will feel confident about reaching for jobs in those areas. Also, more colleges will prepare students for

jobs through programs of study in the communications arts and sciences.

• To deal with competition for jobs in these areas, many people will prepare in *several* areas, to maximize their opportunities.

Interactive (Two-way) Technologies

Probably the most successful interactive technological tool is the telephone, and now that the phone is computerized, the industry is more active than ever. With more than 183 million telephones, Americans make over 800 million phone calls a day.

American Telephone and Telegraph (AT&T), the largest company in the world, was recently divested of its regional subsidiaries and, in exchange, was permitted to compete in new technological areas. Those areas include fire-alert systems, cordless phones, pocket medical transmitters, paging devices, car (mobile) telephones, video-screen information retrieval systems, and a worldwide transmission network known as Integrated Services Digital Network (ISDN). Telephone companies are involved with computer technology almost as much as communications technologies. AT&T Information Systems (the company's new name) will continue to be a new-technology leader and a massive employer.

Teleshopping will continue to increase as new communications/computer technologies "do the walking" for us. More customers will order goods by phone or video-screen. As more women work full time, less time is left for leisurely shopping. As banking-machine technology moves into retail stores, many financial institutions will be merchandise vendors. Thus, employers will tend to be financial/investment companies, linked to others, such as Warner Amex, a combination of Warner Communications Inc. and American Express Company.

Videotext will provide home shopping, along with other services. Videotext connects the television set to a central computer, enabling a subscriber to use a small keyboard for banking, shopping, doing research, playing games, and watching the news. Companies investing in this technology include Knight-Ridder, Times-Mirror, Dow Jones, Reader's Digest, CBS, AT&T, and J. C. Penney.

With the television set connected to a central computer, many people will be able to use the following types of service:

Agricultural market information
News/weather

Home banking/shopping
Electronic mail
Business news/information

Another interactive arena is the video game market. Key companies include CBS/Gabriel Toys and Atari. These surged in popularity in the early 1980s but have dropped sharply in consumer sales (and price). More than 30 million homes are equipped with games. Interactive educational games will no doubt continue to be significant in designing new interactive learning materials (computer-aided instruction, or CAI) in the years ahead. Textbook manufacturers continue to explore this market potential.

Perhaps the most staggering new-technology tool (potential rather than actual) is the videodisc. Using laser technology, the videodisc player permits random-access interaction with program material. When linked with a computer's storage capacity, the disc allows the storage of an entire encyclopedia or museum for visual retrieval. Up to 108,000 individual pictures can be mixed with graphics, animation, or text. This technology is not moving rapidly as a consumer product, but for business and institutional use it has enormous potential. That is especially true for personalized training materials, where "branching" allows a person to move through instructional materials and restudy items if he gives the wrong answer. Major companies include Pioneer, North American Phillips, RCA, General Electric, Sony, and others.

A new-technology consumer surprise has been the personal computer (PC). Figure 7 shows the increase in sales in just three years, and further dramatic growth is expected.

1983: 8.4 million
1984: 15.9 million
1985: 22 million

TAKING
HOMES
BY STORM
Source: The Yankee Group

COURTESY CHANNELS OF COMMUNICATION

Fig. 7.

The parts of the computer (keyboard, disc drives, printer, TV monitor) all process information from, or to, the silicon chip microprocessor. The software program (instructions) tells the computer what to do; when the PC is connected by telephone modem to information outside the home, the user can interact with other PC users in an electronic mail system or as information databases. Computers are also key elements in home security systems. For security, many homes will be hooked into monitoring systems connected to central computers and police or fire departments.

Two other major interactive technologies should be considered because of their job impact: videoconferencing and robotics.

Videoconferences allow people at sites all over the country (or the world) to be interconnected by satellite and telephone technologies. It is estimated that every day 20 million meetings are held in the United States, and 90 percent of air travel is business travel. Some 80 percent of all meetings last less than thirty minutes, and 60 percent of all meetings could be handled by voice communication technologies. Now people can travel to a nearby hotel conference room and attend a meeting, saving long-distance travel time and costs. The video is transmitted from one source and received on large screens at the multiple locations; two-way audio provides live feedback.

Robots, on the other hand, represent a new-technology computerized item (a mechanical system, with flexible motions and intelligence functions) that can impact job opportunities in communications. Although the automobile industry is leading the way in the use of robots, in less than twenty years it is predicted that robots could be performing the equivalent of 2.3 million jobs.

Storage Technologies—Career Choices

All communications delivery systems (radio, television stations, cable systems, and VCRs, for example) must *deliver something*. In most cases they deliver programs: films, video, or computer information. The planning, production, and sale of all this program information represent a major communications career area. This is called the "software" side of the field, as opposed to the machinery, or hardware. Listed below are various communications companies and the types of job activities they offer.

Company	*Job Activities*
Entertainment and Sports Programming Network (ESPN)	Sports; business news

Cox	Storer Communications	Metromedia	Tele-Communications Inc. (TCI)	Viacom	Times Mirror	Tribune Co.	Warner Communications	Turner Broadcasting Co.	Taft
$537.6	$458.9	$371.6	$347.3	$271.3	$270.1	$259.0	$219.0	$201.3	$140.8
87.5%	100%	69.7%	94%	86.0%	66.9%	88.1%	7.3%	89.7%	37.0%
			*Black Entertainment Television	*Lifetime		WGN, WPIX, *AP News Plus	MTV, Nickelodeon	CNN, CNN Headline News, WTBS, CMC	*Black Entertainment Television
*First Ticket, *Bravo, American Movie Classics			Data Cable Express *Event TeleVision (pay-per-view)	*Showtime, *The Movie Channel			*Showtime, *The Movie Channel, *Event TeleVision		
TeleRep	Storer Communications	Metromedia Producers Corp., Metromedia Television	National Telefilms Associates, *TCI/Taft Programs	Viacom Productions		Tribune Entertainment	Warner Bros., Warner Bros. TV	Turner Program Services	Taft Entertainment Co., *TCI/Taft Programs
				Viacom Enterprises			Warner Home Video		Worldvision Enterprises
	Cable Protection Systems			Viacom Worldwide			*Warner Amex Qube		
Indax Videotex			Teletext Services Inc.		Gateway Videotex	Video-Guide Teletext			Electra Teletext
		Metromedia Producers Corp.		Viacom Enterprises		Tribune Entertainment	Warner Bros. TV	Turner Program Services	
		Texas State (1 network)						CNN Radio Network	
5 VHF, 2 UHF	5 VHF, 2 UHF	4 VHF, 3 UHF		3 VHF, 1 UHF	5 VHF, 2 UHF	3 VHF, 2 UHF	5 VHF, 1 UHF	1 UHF	5 VHF, 2 UHF
Cox Cable (3.1)	Storer Cable (2.8)		TCI Cable (4.7)	Viacom Cable (1.4)	Times Mirror Cable (1.8)	Tribune Cable (.098)	*Warner Amex Cable (2.6)		*TCI/Taft Cablevision Associates (.098)
Westar 4, 5 Telstar 301			Westar 5	Galaxy 1 Satcom 3R, 5			Satcom 3R, 4	Satcom 3R Galaxy 1 Westar 3, 4	Westar 5
5 AM, 7 FM		5 AM, 6 FM		2 AM, 5 FM		3 AM, 2 FM			6 AM, 7 FM

COURTESY CHANNELS OF COMMUNICATION

Company	Job Activities
Cable News Network (CNN)	News; features
Cable Satellite Public Affairs Network (C-SPAN)	U.S. House of Representatives coverage; government events/ debates
Nashville Network	Country-oriented entertainment
Learning Channel	Telecourses; how-to programs
Spanish International Network (SIN)	News, entertainment in Spanish
Music Television (MTV)	Video version of radio rock

An Overview and Summary

To review specific job possibilities in distribution, interactive information services, and programming, the best summary is the accompanying chart from *Channels* magazine's *Field Guide to the Electronic Media*. This magazine-edition guide appears annually and represents one of the best brief overviews of telecommunications media. Write to: *Channels*, 304 West 58th Street, New York, NY 10019.

At the top of the chart, the major companies are listed, with total revenue in millions, to guide in job searches. A careful study of the chart will show the subsidiary groups from each large firm and the area of telecommunications in which each is involved. Every company or subsidiary represents a potential telecommunications employer.

Chapter III

The Excitement of Electronic Media

No other industry permeates our lives more than the electronic media. Perhaps that is why these fields attract so many job applicants. The competition for employment is keen.

In 1984 revenues in broadcast television alone exceeded $18 billion; more than the three major networks shared $8 billion of that revenue. Ninety-nine percent of all American homes receive programming either over the air or by cable. Young Americans put in more time watching television than all the hours they spend in classrooms.

In this chapter general categories and specific job areas will be reviewed, including television, radio, new technologies (cable and computers, for example), news, production, media management, sales, corporate media, and opportunities for technicians.

In addition, major career resources and related organizations and agencies are listed for your career planning.

Introduction

Job opportunities in broadcasting are expected to grow by 15 to 27 percent by 1990. More than 1,000 television stations and more than 10,000 radio stations are in operation in the United States. The accompanying table specifies the job areas in various career categories so that you can locate areas that are of special interest and match your particular talents and skills to the job area.

ELECTRONIC MEDIA

Career Categories	Specific Job Areas
TELEVISION/RADIO	
Networks	Affiliate relations; broadcast standards and practices; market research; creative program development; news; sports

Career Categories	Specific Job Areas
Programming/Production	Executive producer; producer; production assistant; director; announcer; host; lighting director; film/video editor; performer; commercials; program manager; floor manager; graphic artist; scenic designer; continuity writer; gaffer; creative/documentary writers; audio control; cameraperson; disc jockey; researcher; special effects; musicians
News	Reporter; anchor; news analyst/commentator; interviewer; news director; assignment editor; researcher; arts critic; weatherperson; sports anchor; rewriter; stringer; writer; investigative reporter
Engineering	Maintenance engineer; transmitter specialist; mobile technician; antenna/microwave specialist; factory service rep; service manager; installation serviceman; chief engineer; broadcast technician
Sales/Management	General manager; business manager; sales rep; promotion manager; traffic manager; public service/community affairs director; copywriter
CORPORATE MEDIA	Programming/production personnel (see above); technical specialists; audiovisual coodinators; teleconference coordinator; promotion experts
NEW TECHNOLOGIES	Cable access representatives; customer service reps; computer/interactive experts; satellite technicians; telephone technicians

Two publications track the field for those interested: *Broadcasting* magazine and *Variety*. Serious job-hunters study both to keep informed of changes and opportunities.

One of the most valuable concepts to keep in mind is that of networking. Everyone is familiar with the three major TV networks, but networking, the process of making job contacts, is basic to life in the electronic-media job world.

Jobs at the major networks, CBS, NBC, and ABC, are scarce, but many other opportunities exist: radio networks or interconnections, public broadcasting links, regional networks in cable, even computer networking will provide new career fields in the future. And to repeat, one must network with people to form the vital links that lead to jobs.

Keep in mind also that the heart of the broadcasting and electronic world is the *program*. It has been said that people don't watch TV stations or satellite transmissions; they watch programs. So good program production leads to success. Even if you are not interested in doing production, your own role in media will depend upon some creative production skills.

The electronic media offer many options. Two that are often overlooked are the noncommercial options and the whole area of sound. Remember that in addition to the commercial broadcasting world (or the corporate media opportunities), many nonprofit groups such as schools, colleges, hospitals, and government agencies employ media professionals. People tend to think of video exclusively, but there are dramatic changes and opportunities in audio, such as stereo television, digital recordings, and others.

Advice from Professionals

The National Association of Broadcasters, the industry's major trade group, says that personal characteristics such as diligence, honesty, and loyalty are of course important, but it cites others as well. Enthusiasm is helpful, because the field is fast-paced. Creativity is a basic necessity, since the "product" sold in broadcasting is a creative program package. Other important traits are reliability (meeting deadlines), initiative, a balanced temperament, and a sense of public relations and good business.

There are many routes or avenues into the broadcasting world. One is the "Go-fer" route ("Go-fer a cup of coffee"); cheerfully doing menial jobs can lead to good opportunities after you get *inside* the field. Many people learn a lot by serving as production assistants or technical assistants.

One of the best ways to gain experience is through participation in an internship program. Such opportunities, offered by many colleges and universities, permit students to learn on the job while earning credits toward a degree. A hard-working intern can turn an unpaid internship into a paid position after schooling is completed.

One may get a broadcasting position by working for production companies that make either long productions or sixty-second commercials. Many people gain experience in these somewhat smaller operations and then move on to larger TV stations or networks.

Women who want to work in media positions need to form special networks among themselves. In the *Columbia Journalism Review*, one professional states: "In the old days women turned on each other; now we turn *to* each other." Today women are in charge of 8 percent of TV newsrooms and 18 percent of radio newsrooms. More than one third of all news anchors are women. The Corporation for Public Broadcasting supports special training grants for women and members of minority groups. Several organizations help women find jobs: American

Women in Radio and Television, Women in Communications, and Women in Cable.

In large media operations jobs tend to be specialized, whereas in small stations people do many jobs. That permits a person to gain experience in a wide range of media tasks.

In a recent *Careers Research Monograph* published by the Institute for Research in Chicago, several professionals described their jobs.

A Radio Announcer

I am an announcer for a large radio station located near a major city. I am part of a team of broadcasters responsible for programming at this station. I had a master's degree in journalism and several years' experience in radio before I got this job.

[Earlier, at a smaller station,] I filed recordings, scripts, and other papers, answered the phone, and pulled copy printed on the news machine [news from the wire services] and gave it to the announcer on the air. I ran errands and did anything that was needed. But I was learning: about commercial procedures, equipment, and management, mostly by observation.

COURTESY EMERSON COLLEGE

Women are finding their way into TV news operations.

A News Reporter

I work for a major TV station. I am a news reporter, functioning as part of a news team. The most visible persons on the team are the anchor, co-anchor, news analyst, sports commentator, and weather forecaster. There are several news reporters like myself. We usually work in the field, to cover on-the-spot news. When we do this, we appear on the screen too.

I had my bachelor's degree in journalism and was working on my master's when I made my first appearance on TV, at another sta-

Staff announcers handle varied assignments on small stations.

tion. I'd had considerable print and other experience before I was hired by this station.

I always knew I'd be a writer. I had published in newspapers and teen magazines before I was out of high school.

JOB CATEGORIES

Television

There's no doubt that the excitement and glamour of television capture the interest of young people.

The TV industry is based for the most part on commercial advertising, which determines the nature of the industry: its competitive nature, its need for large audiences to support advertising dollars spent, and even its news operations.

In such fields there is tremendous turnover among personnel. Some people simply burn out because of the pace and pressures.

People in TV must face competition for their jobs. Hard work is essential in the industry. Another given is irregular hours. Stations are on the air throughout the day and evening hours.

One less well-known part of the industry is research, upon which the entire field of television is based. Audience and market research (which produces "the ratings") is central to financial success. Highly sophisticated techniques are used to test the market for program series and to identify segments of the audience that view particular programs (enabling advertisers to buy appropriate audiences for their products). Thus, persons with a scientific/statistical bent may find a satisfying niche in this aspect of television.

A variety of "markets" are available for television careers: large TV stations in metropolitan areas may employ up to 250 people; a small-city station may employ about 30. Most stations have four divisions of activity: administration, programming, engineering, and sales. News operations may come under programming or may be a separate operation because of the increasing importance of news (both from a programming and an advertising/sales point of view).

Radio

Radio stations may be independent or affiliated with a national or regional network. *Broadcasting Yearbook* is the main directory of radio and TV stations in the United States. It gives call letters, addresses, names of management, and the station's format, such as jazz, classical or popular music, all-news, or all-sports.

People interested in radio jobs can gain experience either in a station run by the college they attend or at a small station that uses volunteers. There are also national network training programs for outstanding students. The Broadcast Education Association is an organization of 200 schools and colleges that offer courses in radio and television.

New Technologies: Cable, Satellites, Computers

As new communications technologies develop, people are finding wider opportunities in the electronic media. In fields such as cable television, inexperienced people can develop successful careers rapidly. However, companies operating in new-technology fields are subject to changes and risks; some grow and some fail in an uncertain marketplace. Yet one should examine these areas carefully for career opportunities. Women, for example, are finding it easy to move ahead in the sales departments of cable companies. The computer is important to the development of most new communications technologies. It is important to become computer literate.

Programming/Production

The planning, creation, and production of "shows" represent the lifeblood of broadcasting and of many new technologies as well. Many communications careers are available in this area.

Local programs are produced by station staff in a variety of formats: children's shows, religious programs, interview programs, panel shows, teen-age programs, sports events, and public affairs. Programs such as films, drama, comedy, and game shows are also produced by independent producers and syndication companies.

Programming involves a wide variety of job areas. Producers conceptualize and develop the shows and production details; directors "call the shots" when actual production takes place; and numerous people back up the production team: lighting experts, editors, floor managers, graphic artists, scenic designers, writers, audio and camera personnel, special effects experts.

The program director determines and administers programming policies, in conjunction with the general manager and the sales manager. Stations also utilize production managers, producers, and directors for programming. Staff announcers read commercial copy, introduce programs (live and taped), and give station identifications along with public service announcements.

News

News production is a separate division at some stations. The public's increasing appetite for news has created new career opportunities. A news operation can be extremely profitable, and thus there is keen competition among stations. As in all good broadcasting production, writers are key to a good news operation. Other key positions include reporter, anchor, news analyst/commentator, interviewer, news director, assignment editor, weather and sports persons, and investigative reporter.

News can be presented in a variety of formats—local, regional, national, international—and the locale for the news reporter varies according to the focus. CBS reporter Charles Kuralt often travels around the United States in a mobile cruiser searching for and filming news features to broadcast on the network. Many correspondents worldwide feed news features from the scene, interpreting events and cultures to Americans.

An interesting political and economic reality is the development of the idea of a "new world information order." This concept suggests that reporting on less-developed nations be more balanced, allowing more control over news coverage.

New technologies have altered the character of news in recent years. Satellite technology makes it possible to interconnect worldwide news operations. Television cameras and recorders are now mobile, making it possible to broadcast live news from the scene. Persons who plan a career in news should be prepared to work at the center of action and in sometimes dangerous newsmaking events.

In the future, news will be transmitted to the home in print on television screens. By use of a dial system through a telephone, viewers will be able to obtain news features of their choice, whether international, business, or local news.

Since people will not read long features on a television screen, special writing techniques are needed for this new transmission format. Gannett is a company involved in this development. Its newspaper *USA Today* demonstrates the kind of news writing with color graphics that will be featured.

Even if these new news forms do not spread widely, there is no doubt that the computer will permeate news work. Many papers and magazines are already produced by satellite transmission to printing plants. Many newsrooms have terminals instead of typewriters. Persons interested in news careers must be computer literate.

One final point: Most professionals insist that *writing*, good writing, is the essence of journalistic success. A background in history and economics provides the factual and analytical skills required of a good journalist.

Engineering

In most stations technical personnel are supervised by a chief engineer, who understands the operation and maintenance of technical equipment. He often holds a First Class Radio Telephone Operator's license and is familiar with the rules and regulations of the Federal Communications Commission (FCC).

Broadcast technicians—audio and video engineers—work with the chief engineer to operate and maintain the station's electronic equipment. These people usually perform a full range of production, maintenance, and repair jobs. A high school diploma and technical or trade school courses are minimum requirements for these positions. Many college students gain engineering "know-how" by working in college radio and TV studios. Internships are another way to gain hands-on experience in engineering.

One of the challenges of engineering today is the rapid pace of change in broadcasting equipment resulting from silicon chip technology. Engineers need to keep abreast of these changes to help stations stay current with new technologies.

Sales

Radio and television stations earn revenue from the sale of advertising time on the local, regional, and national levels. In large stations, a sales staff makes calls and presentations to local accounts. Sales personnel also develop new advertising accounts for media outlets. Courses such as advertising, marketing, broadcasting, and psychology are valuable in training for sales positions. Pay is often both fixed salary and commission, so an enthusiastic person can earn an excellent income in media sales.

The traffic department usually operates in conjunction with the sales department. These people prepare daily schedules that guide the minute-by-minute broadcasting service. All information concerning programs and commercials is organized by the traffic manager. Another position is that of continuity director, who is in charge of writing and producing commercial announcements for the sales department.

Management in Media

The business management and administrative work in radio and television stations is under the direction of a general manager, often a person who has been successful in sales, programming, or engineering. The manager consults with the program manager, sales manager, and chief engineer. He or she usually handles the station's relations with the FCC and other government bodies and participates in community activities on behalf of the station.

The financial department is headed by a controller or business manager, who oversees financial transactions and prepares the necessary reports. This person usually supervises personnel and labor relations and general housekeeping activities at the station.

Organizations that own several stations have a headquarters staff that specializes in finance, law, and labor relations.

In addition to broadcasting roles, many other media opportunities are linked to management. Cable companies and other new-technology firms offer management opportunities for persons whose interest and expertise bridge the media and the financial/management worlds.

The world of corporate media represents an opportunity for persons interested in media production in a business setting. Corporate media activities are often linked to top management, since media staffers work with the corporate image.

Corporate media personnel produce video training materials for corporate personnel; for example, for computer salesmen who need to keep up-to-date on products. Corporations today produce more video programs than all three television networks combined. It is estimated that AT&T spends more money educating its personnel than the entire budget of Massachusetts Institute of Technology.

In summary, many career opportunities exist in electronic media: networks, programming/production, news, engineering, sales/management, and corporate media.

The world of electronic media is an exciting world. Its challenges are met by people who are academically well prepared and who work hard to stay on top of a rapidly changing technological environment.

Chapter IV

The Power of the Print Media

It is estimated that 85 percent of the communications industries involves written and print communications. Book publishing, for example, exceeds $7 billion in sales annually from the sale of over 40,000 titles, one quarter of which are textbooks.

More than 500 publishing firms operate in the United States alone. More than 9,000 newspapers, more than 5,000 general-circulation magazines, and 12,000 trade magazines are published, with a combined circulation of 60 million.

The career options for the person interested in print media include creative and professional writing, book publishing, editing, marketing, new technologies in publishing, special-interest publishing, and journalism.

Advice from the Professionals

Persons interested in writing and publishing need to know the skills, personality characteristics, and type of education necessary for a career in print media. According to the professionals, they should:

- Acquire good oral skills
- Be precise
- Be open to new ideas
- Keep up with current events
- Be able to take criticism
- Be original and relevant
- Do independent research
- Become familiar with electronic equipment
- Start writing in high school and college
- Work for school newspapers and yearbooks
- Concentrate on small papers for the first job

Students should take English composition courses, with emphasis on spelling, vocabulary, etymology, and literature. Typing is also highly recommended.

In high school one should concentrate on creative writing, journalism, speech, and drama. In college a broad liberal arts education is a good preparation for the print media.

Many people interested in careers in print media take a college degree in journalism or creative writing, supplemented by relevant electives.

Key journalism courses include history and principles of journalism, American and foreign press, communications law, news evaluation, reporting, copy editing, and reporting of public affairs.

Many who study writing or journalism in college also prepare themselves for advertising and public relations careers. Coursework in those areas might include principles and practices of advertising, ad copy, psychology in advertising, salesmanship, advertising campaigns, newspaper promotion, radio-TV advertising, public relations, and business communications.

In a recent Careers Research Monograph published by the Institute for Research, "Writing for Television and Radio," several professional writers describe their work.

Dramatic Script Writer

I write drama TV. I've been doing this for some time. I got my degree in liberal arts, a degree in journalism, and had a lot of other writing experience before I started writing for TV.

"Scribbling" was my chief source of "pure joy" for as far back as I can remember. I was a scribbler of words before I entered kindergarten. I am a firm believer that real writers are born writers.

In high school, I took journalism, creative writing, and was editor of the school paper. I won or placed in a number of contests, sold articles to newspapers, and short stories to magazines that ran special departments for teen-age scribes.

Radio Continuity Writer

I write straight continuity and other original materials for several radio stations. I took courses in writing at a community college.

Disc jockeys read my stuff between recordings, announcements, and other programs. I do not have to follow any particular writing format. I write as I would any other piece, concisely and to the point, but tailor my writing to a conversational style.

Radio Commercial Writer

I write commercials for radio stations. I had two years' college education, some writing talent, and the "yen" to put that talent to use when I began this work.

As I turned the radio dial I thought some of the commercials sounded pretty good; but others—well, I thought I could do better. I learned to think commercials. I learned to be imaginative and original. I learned the limitations of the sixty-second, thirty-second, and ten-second commercial, as these are bounded by the number of words that can be used.

Science Documentary Writer

I majored in science in college and the summer after graduation participated in a three-month field trip to search for ancient remains of an American Indian tribe. I followed the filming closely and made extensive notes and records of everything.

I have pursued my love of science and exploration with a simultaneous fascination with the possibilities of television for communicating the job of discovering ancient and new truths about people and the universe. I am on staff now with the station and am scheduled for a one-hour documentary special every month.

These comments convey a variety of backgrounds and tasks among professionals. Some specific jobs in print media are the following:

Book Publishing

Publishing careers involve the production and sale of books, magazines, and newspapers. Publishing includes the selection of works for publication, the editing of those works, the processes of layout, design, and printing, the marketing and advertising of the publication, the management of the publishing firm, and the circulation of published materials.

PRINT MEDIA

Career Categories	Specific Job Areas
BOOK/MAGAZINE PUBLISHING	Production manager; production staff; traffic and distribution director; art director; managing editor; book designer; sales rep; illustrator; authors; children's book editor (see also, all editorial listings below)

Career Categories	Specific Job Areas
EDITORS	Sponsoring book editor; editing supervisor; acquisitions editor; editorial assistant; associate editor; senior editor; staff writer; copy editor; art director; fashion editor; managing editor; editor-in chief; news editor; city editor; foreign editors; wire editors; make up editor; copy writer/editor; proofreader
NEWSPAPERS	(Editorial positions, listed above); weather reporter; bureau chief; cartoonist; political analyst; newspaper circulation manager; sports staff writer; classified and advertising manager; specialists/writers; subscription manager; circulation marketing director; stringers; staff writers; freelancers; reporters (general, special, beat); foreign news correspondent; wire service coordinator; business/finance editor
ADVERTISING	Business forecaster; trade show coordinator; advertising sales rep; sales manager; research director; advertising sales director; publicity director; copywriter; marketing director; art director; copy supervisor; creative director; graphic/commercial artist; media buyer/director; production coordinator; announcer; cartoonist; market identification expert; research staff
PUBLIC RELATIONS	Lobbying coordinator; news conference/news release director; community relations director; personnel information coordinator; political campaign manager; brochure designer; audio-visual coordinator; government relations director; product information/promotion coordinator; newsletter editor; college publications coordinator; speechwriter; employee publications manager; training films director; fund-raising coordinator; consumer affairs coordinator
SPECIAL PRINT FIELDS	Catalogue designer; mail order sales director; technical illustrator; aeronautics/aerospace writer; computer expert (writing); data management coordinator of publications; instructional manual writer; petroleum/energy specialist; pharmaceutical industry writer; programmed instruction writer; technical trade publications coordinator; medical publications writer/coordinator; electronic writing specialist

Guide to Careers in Book Publishing, published by the McGraw-Hill Book Company, contains helpful information about the career. It also points out that today's publisher may deal with several media besides books: films, audio and video tapes, transparencies, phonograph records, and filmstrips.

The most familiar type of book publishing is the publication of general books (called "trade books" because they are sold to the general public by the publishing trade). Children's books represent a significant segment of trade book publishing. Children's books may be science fiction, books about sports figures or other heroes or heroines, books on nature, dictionaries, how-to books, and science books.

Another significant sector of book publishing is professional publishing: books for doctors, lawyers, scientists, engineers, or other professionals. They are often circulated through special-interest book clubs or specialized bookstores.

Educational publishing accounts for a major percentage of book sales each year. Nearly 50 million students are enrolled in public and private elementary and secondary schools, and more than 10 million students in two- and four-year colleges. Another 30 million students are enrolled in evening schools or on-the-job training programs in factories, offices and stores, and in home-study courses. Their learning materials consist of textbooks, workbooks, and laboratory manuals. But many other instructional materials are also published: films, filmstrips, cards and charts, and language laboratory materials.

The book publishing field encompasses a variety of jobs. That of the book designer is one. The designer is responsible for the total "look" of the book. He or she selects typefaces, chooses colors, supervises drawings and artwork, and plans the layout and the cover of the book, all with the goal of making the book attractive and easy to use. This role allows for a lot of creativity, not just with the printed word, but with the total design of a published work.

The production of a book requires a production supervisor, who arranges the composition, printing, binding, and packaging of books. He or she begins work when a book is being planned and represents the publisher in dealings with manufacturers: printers, binders, paper suppliers, and many others. Supervisors need to have a thorough knowledge of the printing business. Most have studied graphic arts.

Another interesting career in book publishing is marketing. Usually people begin as sales representatives and move into marketing positions.

Sales representatives often travel to conventions or trade shows where books, especially textbooks, are promoted and advertised. Trade books are sold to bookstores or to wholesalers. A schoolbook representative is often an educational service specialist for the publisher. He or she is often a learning specialist and knows the latest ideas in education, providing valuable ideas to publishers. Sometimes a sales representative becomes an editor and works into a top editorial/management job.

Editors

Editors work in the development of ideas for books and in finding authors to write them. However, an editor's work also involves sponsoring a certain segment of a publishing venture. Such an editor may be called a senior editor, a project editor, or a product development manager.

A sponsoring editor proposes a book for publication, selects the author, and supervises the development of the product from the idea stage to the finished project. The actual scope of the sponsoring editor's responsibility depends on the size of the market and the breadth of the publisher's coverage.

A sponsoring editor must have a "feel" for marketing, along with some experience in publishing. Sponsoring editors in educational publishing may have been members of the publishing sales staff or may have been teachers.

The position of sponsoring editor is often a good career step toward a management position in publishing.

Another editorial job is that of editing supervisor. This person works with the manuscript through the stages of production until the actual manufacture of the book begins. He or she works with authors, encourages them to improve their writing, and keeps the publication project on a time schedule.

Still another editorial role is copy editor, the person who goes over the manuscript meticulously to make certain that every sentence is clear and grammatically correct.

Another stage in publishing involves proofreading the manuscript after it has been set in type. Usually the galley proofs are read by the author and by the publisher's proofreader, who look for typographical errors. Proofreaders sometimes work on a free-lance basis.

On a newspaper the editor has overall editorial supervision of the entire paper, and he or she often writes editorials for the paper. Other newspaper editorial jobs include:

- News editor, who allocates space for news items
- Managing editor, who oversees editorial functions
- City editor, who directs and gathers local news and supervises reporters, photographers, and rewriters
- Foreign editor, who is in charge of international news
- Copy editor, who is in charge of all copyreaders as they check grammar, punctuation, and style and write headlines
- Department editors, who edit special sections such as sports and women's pages

- Production editors, who manage all mechanical aspects of production

Obviously, the work of editors is varied and specialized; in many ways the final product is the result of editorial supervision.

Publishing and Technology

New career fields are being opened up in print media by electronic advances, usually called "electronic publishing." Print media fields are being altered significantly by these new telecommunications technologies.

Print businesses are growing by about 11 percent annually, but electronic products are developing at more than 25 percent each year. Information in computerized form is now a $3.2 billion annual business.

Publishers use computer and communications technologies to automate production of their publications. Many newspaper and magazine articles are currently edited on computers. The *Wall Street Journal* and *USA Today* send their publications by satellite to their printing plants in various parts of the country.

Many publishers are considering other information distribution possibilities such as the delivery of news and information directly to the TV screen or personal computer. The advantage of such information distribution is in its interactive nature: You can talk back to the video "printed page" by requesting more information or by responding or selecting your information according to your own specialized needs.

One of the most interesting examples of an electronic publishing product is the News Retrieval Service of Dow Jones & Company, which distributes financial information. Another is the Nexis service of Mead Corporation's Mead Data Central. Another service, Chemical Abstracts, prints abstracts of research papers and patents.

Some of the major companies that are entering the electronics publishing field are:

Merrill Lynch Pierce Fenner & Smith, Inc.
Sears Roebuck & Co.
Knight-Ridder News, Inc.
Citicorp
Dun & Bradstreet Corporation
Gannett Company
A. C. Nielsen & Company

Scholastic, Inc.
Simon & Schuster, Inc.
Prentice-Hall, Inc.
McGraw-Hill Book Company

Electronic publishing, however, is not expected to replace print. Prentice-Hall, for example, sold over $15 million in books about personal computers in one year. Thus, even new technologies require print materials to explain what they are about.

Journalism

The term "journalism" was once limited to the profession of writing for newspapers and magazines. Today journalists work in broadcasting, for public relations firms or departments, for advertising agencies, for public affairs departments of schools, colleges, and other nonprofit organizations, and for government agencies. Journalists work primarily as reporters, feature writers, specialist writers, editors, critics, and copywriters. Other jobs include sports editor, movie critic, classified and advertising editor, financial editor, foreign correspondent, and weather reporter.

Most Americans receive their news in thirty- and sixty-second time slots on television; but for in-depth coverage of events—local, national, and international—many turn to the newspaper.

In the past decade, Watergate and new technologies have altered career opportunities in the newspaper. The Watergate revelations (and the Hollywood treatment of the reporters Woodward and Bernstein) attracted thousands of young people to journalism studies. Each year these graduates compete fiercely for positions.

Newsrooms and back rooms look different today than they did in the past. Typewriters have been replaced by video display terminals (VDTs), which allow writing and editing to be done electronically.

However, reporters still gather news in the time-honored way. To cover a story, they gather all necessary facts, by interviews, research, news sources, and other means. The reporter then returns to the newsroom, writes the story usually to an assigned length, and sends the copy to the desk editor. Or the reporter may phone all the details to a rewriter, who will write the story.

In the early 1980s the Newspaper Fund Gallup Survey of Journalism Graduates indicated that virtually all of the nation's 166,000 journalism and communications graduates who actively looked for media work were employed within six months after they finished college.

Daily newspapers took 10.4 percent of the graduates; public relations employed 8.9 percent; advertising hired 8.5 percent; TV stations took 8.8 percent; radio stations, 5.5 percent; weekly newspapers, 4.7 percent; and commercial magazines 2.8 percent. The nonmedia fields of sales, management, clerical work, and others attracted a quarter of the graduates, 27.3 percent.

More than 75 percent of the graduates who majored in broadcast news or production found jobs on radio and television stations, and nearly 60 percent of the advertising and public relations majors found jobs in their fields.

Nearly 80 percent of those who landed jobs on daily or weekly newspapers specialized in news/editorial studies, and an additional 15 percent of the news majors chose public relations or advertising jobs to begin their careers.

Incidentally, record numbers of women and minority group members are graduating from journalism programs. Women made up 61.6 percent of the class in 1980, compared to 59.6 percent a year earlier and 46.6 percent five years earlier. Minority group members represented 8.8 percent of the graduating class, compared to 8.1 percent a year earlier and 5.5 percent five years earlier.

The Institute for Career Research reports the following variety of experiences reported by journalists:

Journalist A

Over the years I have employed many beginning reporters. Although some first-class reporters have had only a high school education, they were extremely talented and exceedingly interested, with a driving desire to become good journalists.

Basically, even those having college education must have the above qualities too. Other qualifications I want from my reporters include a good command of English and ability to write. You'd be surprised at how many can't spell!

Journalist B

I am a sports nut. I always have been. At school I liked to play baseball, basketball, and ice hockey. I also liked to write about them. I could write better than I could play.

Once out of school, I covered all local games for the local press. But greener pastures beckoned. A larger paper made me an offer I couldn't refuse.

Journalist C

I am the editor of a small-town biweekly newspaper. We have a business manager, three reporters, a switchboard operator-clerk, an ad sales person, and an assistant editor. The printing is done by another, larger paper for a fee. As editor, I not only handle employee relations but cover some community affairs and events. I always take along a camera and double as photographer. I fill in on other jobs too.

Journalist D

I am an overseas news correspondent for a major U.S. paper. As a correspondent I've met and interviewed top politicians, entertainers, athletes, scientists, astronauts, famous painters, authors, and other notable and influential persons.

Whenever there has been a major happening anywhere in the world these past few years, I've often been one of the correspondents sent from our bureau to cover the story. Sometimes it's been thrilling. Sometimes appalling or terrifying. Sometimes it is easy to analyze and report what's happening. Sometimes it has taken all my intuition, initiative, experience, and courage to discover the really relevant facts and transmit them to my newspaper.

The above excerpts illustrate the variety of journalism careers and their very different challenges. College journalism programs offer an equally wide variety of courses to help prepare you for widely disparate demands. Among them are:

- History of journalism
- Censorship in totalitarian societies
- Law and the press
- Reporting
- Public affairs reporting
- News writing
- News editing
- Editorial management
- Editorial writing
- Foreign news reporting
- Television and radio journalism
- Magazine writing, editing, and publishing
- Magazine feature writing

- Technical writing
- Research methods
- Photojournalism
- Graphic arts

Many journalists work with national and international news reporting services. Two of the largest are United Press International (UPI) and Associated Press (AP). UPI is a commercial news service. Many newspapers, newsmagazines, and TV and radio stations subscribe to its service both here and abroad. The AP is owned by various news publications and some TV and radio stations as a cooperative organization. It maintains bureaus in many cities both in the U.S. and overseas.

In conclusion, the following are suggestions from a cross section of working journalists:

- Take political science and government courses
- Know how to use a 35mm camera and develop film
- Gain working experience on a college paper
- Try to get an internship
- Consider your first job as your fifth year of college
- Be persistent and patient
- Don't overlook job opportunities on small weeklies
- If you can't find a job, take one in a related field while waiting for an opening.

Remember, too, that the growth of computer technology means greater streamlining of technical operations within news companies, from accounting to page production. The need is great for talented production managers with technical and news/editorial backgrounds. And as newspapers (and videotext news delivery systems) become more graphically appealing, there will be a need for young people with skills in layout, photography, and art design to produce news pages that are attractive and easy to read.

Special Print Fields

Outside of journalism or consumer publications, many other writing/print job opportunities exist. One large area is the "trade press," magazines, newspapers, and newsletters addressed to industry, professional, and technical audiences. According to the American Business

Press, there are more than 2,300 such publications, publishing some 63 million copies collectively. The trade press has many more entry-level positions, and advancement can be rapid.

Another advantage of writing for the trade press is that reporting requires more depth in writing than does the consumer press. Also the writer has more influence upon his audience, since readers rely upon trade press information in their field.

A trade publication tends to allow you to combine your interests. If you like science, art, or antiques, all three areas have trade publications.

The major trade publication houses are (all in New York):

Gralla Publications
Lebhar-Friedman
Fairchild Publications
Billboard Publications
R. R. Bowker
Dun and Bradstreet
McGraw-Hill
Ziff-Davis Publishing

A major source of information on trade publications is American Business Press, Inc., 205 East 42nd Street, New York, NY 10017.

One other field of specialty should be mentioned: that of technical writing. Technical writers work for industry, government, and non-profit organizations, translating technological material and facts into understandable language. Technical writers may prepare brochures, manuals, or complex documents and research papers.

One requirement is basic to all print media careers: You must have something to say!

Just as "software packages" make computer technology work, it is the "message" that is the key to all communications in print. The quality of the message will insure success in careers in print.

Chapter V

Communications in Business

W. Charles Redding, considered by some the "father" of business and organization communications, has said, "Communication is the glue that holds an organization together." The facts bear out his statement. Managers spend an overwhelming amount of their time engaged in various communications-related activities. In a survey of human resource executives asked to rank the importance of twenty-four work-related skills, employee communications ranked second in importance.

Some of the communications-related activities in business are:

- Writing public relations releases
- Speaking before groups of employees
- Conducting interviews with employees
- Writing memoranda and all other forms of correspondence
- Training new employees
- Talking with colleagues over lunch
- Engaging in teleconferences with employees in a distant office
- Discussing work-related policies
- Making telephone calls
- Listening to speeches at business luncheons

Evidence suggests that most business and professional employees and managers spend the majority of their work day engaged in one or more of the basic communication activities: speaking, writing, reading, and listening. One study reported that over 48 percent of the average worker's time on the job is spent in *oral* communication. The importance and frequency of communication tends to increase with organizational responsibility. Managers attend more meetings, are asked to speak more often, and are required to write more letters and memos than are their subordinates.

Time is spent providing information, organizing information, and acquiring information. Much of this is done through face-to-face contact. Oral communication is often the preferred means because of its speed and adaptability.

Recent graduates of a large midwestern college of business administration were surveyed to determine the communications skills required of people when they enter a business organization. Their five most important communication skills were:

1. Listening
2. Advising
3. Instructing
4. Routine information exchange
5. Persuading

Business Career Opportunities

If you examine the Sunday classified ads in a newspaper of any large city, you are apt to see some version of the term "communications" mentioned repeatedly. A wide variety of jobs and career options are available for persons with communications degrees.

The following is a list of job titles and career possibilities that have appeared in recent issues of the Boston *Globe*, New York *Times*, *Wall Street Journal*, and *Chronicle of Higher Education*:

Training director	Research associate
Organizational research analyst	Manager of organizational development
Human resource director	Public relations apprentice
Newsletter editor	Advertising agency account executive
Multimedia specialist	Group sales representative
Survey specialist	Communication consultant
Community relations officer	Director of corporate communication
Management trainee	Public opinion researcher
Public relations director	Director of media services
Marketing assistant	Information specialist
Sales coordinator	Sales trainer
Instructional specialist	Media relations assistant
Internal communications director	Internal newsletter editor
Personnel coordinator	Marketing account coordinator
Human relations director	Word processing coordinator

Here we shall focus on the general areas of advertising, marketing and sales, public relations, business media and media production, training and development, and the growing field of computer applications, information management, and word processing.

Advertising

The advertising industry is one of the most exciting and challenging of all the communications industries. Some 4,000 advertising agencies are operating in the United States, employing more than 100,000 people. Job opportunities are expected to grow at a rate of 15 to 27 percent by 1990.

According to the American Association of Advertising Agencies, almost one third of the people involved in advertising work in agencies. The others are involved in media: television, video, radio, magazines, newspapers, outdoor, transit; in the advertising departments of companies; or with suppliers. Advertising jobs include copywriting, art direction, advertising research, video production, graphics, packaging, finance, and retail promotion.

Many people majoring in communications gain experience by working in an advertising agency. The advertising agency is charged with planning, creating, producing, and placing print advertisements and broadcast commercials for its clients. Most of the national print and broadcast advertisements are produced by major advertising agencies. National and local advertising agencies also handle the advertising that is placed in trade, technical, and business publications.

One career description is that of *account executive.* The advertising agency account executive works closely with the client. This person needs to utilize many communications skills, including effective interpersonal communication, persuasion, managerial skills, creativity, and research skills.

The account executive must understand marketing and market analysis and research, management and finance, and sales techniques.

Other career options in advertising are copywriter, media buyer, art director, broadcast video producer, print production representative, and media representative.

The *copywriter* is responsible for creating a text to accompany the print advertisement or the broadcast commercial that will evoke audience response.

The *art director* is responsible for making the visual elements communicate effectively to the audience. The art director is responsible for conceptualizing the ad and selecting and directing the artists and photographers who present the ideas.

The *broadcast video producer* acts as a coordinator with the agency when a broadcast advertisement is being produced. From hiring performers to working with an editor to create the final piece, the producer must have excellent managerial and interpersonal communication skills.

The *media buyer* is responsible for placing the print or broadcast advertisement in newspapers, on radio or television, or on outdoor posters to transit vehicles to achieve the greatest effect.

The *print production representative* is responsible for the mechanical production of all materials that are necessary to the final processing of the advertisement. Some experience in typography, layout, design, and graphic and visual arts is necessary for this job.

People working as *media representatives* or in sales promotion are the salespeople for newspapers, magazines, and broadcast stations. They are familiar with the advantages of their own medium and how it relates to the entire advertising industry. Many successful advertising executives began as media representatives or salespersons.

Marketing and Sales

More than 8 million people are employed in marketing and sales, and job opportunities are expected to increase by 27 to 49 percent by 1990.

It is reported that one quarter to one third of all jobs in the United States are marketing- and sales-related. In addition, many nonprofit organizations (e.g., hospitals, educational institutions, government agencies, and charitable and religious organizations) realize the importance of marketing, and the number of career positions is expanding rapidly.

Many career options are available for communications students interested in marketing and sales.

Market research is one area that is vital to the actual selling of a product or service. Market research is also important to the advertising of the product, idea, innovation, or service.

Marketing researchers are responsible for gathering, assembling, and analyzing data related to the marketing of a product or service. In market research one analyzes the public as consumers: Who are they? What are their attitudes? How do they behave? Why do they do the things they do? Before the sales staff can effectively sell a product or service, it needs an assessment of the potential buyers. That is the major job of the market researcher.

Entry-level market researchers may be responsible for assembling data that has already been published in government documents, sales and accounting records, and other periodicals. As a person becomes better established in the market research area, he or she may be responsible for editing and coding the data obtained from surveys and questionnaires and for the actual conduct of surveys. Marketing surveys take many forms: mail, telephone, personal interview, and direct observational methods.

As one becomes more experienced in market research, his or her responsibilities may also include defining problems and developing hypotheses, designing the methods and procedures for conducting the research, analyzing and interpreting the data, and writing the report.

Advertising agencies also make use of the market research analyst in product research. This particular type of market research investigates how the public relates to a product, idea, or service. Will they buy it? Do they understand how to use it for maximum effectiveness? What characteristics or qualities of the product do they find inviting or annoying?

The greatest number of career opportunities in marketing are in personal sales. Personal sales involves the process of persuading an individual or a group of individuals to purchase a product or service by some means of personal communication. The sales profession encompasses a wide variety of options in the areas of retail, wholesale, and manufacturing sales.

The retail salesperson makes the actual transaction between the retail organization and the consumer. The salesperson needs to have extensive knowledge of the product or products he or she is selling. Sales personnel may need some technical training in selling items such as computers, large appliances, and automobiles. People with retail sales experience often are promoted to positions as buyers, department heads, and managers.

Retail management is another career option. In addition to managing the sales force, retail managers often are involved in selecting and ordering merchandise, handling promotional activities, personnel management, inventory control, and customer credit operations.

A career in wholesale sales might involve assisting customers with sales, sales promotion and publicity, planning and negotiating sales transactions between a vendor and a retailer or consumer; setting prices; and providing customers with technical, management, and marketing assistance.

Manufacturer sales is yet another career option frequently chosen by the communications student. The manufacturing sales representative is responsible for selling a company's product to wholesalers, retailers, and commercial and industrial consumers. Many holders of communications degrees are involved in manufacturing sales with computer firms, pharmaceutical houses, and large high-tech firms such as IBM, Xerox, Digital Equipment, Data General, and Honeywell.

Public Relations

More than 1,200 public relations firms are in operation in the United States, and many advertising firms and other corporations have public relations departments. Some 80,000 persons are employed in the field. Jobs are expected to increase at a rate of 15 to 27 percent by 1990. One of the most exciting, desirable, and fastest-growing of all communications career options, public relations is also one of the most misunderstood. A recent study listed four major misconceptions about the term *public relations*:

1. Public relations is simply press-agentry, the creation of "stunts" that are novel and therefore attract the news media.
2. The public relations practitioner is a smooth-talking, well-connected person who can make things appear better by a few clever manipulations.
3. Public relations is manipulation of people's minds by unethical opportunists who have the ability to make the masses believe things that are not true.
4. Public relations is sheer publicity, getting a particular message into newspapers and magazines or on radio and television.

The article went on to suggest that there is a kernel of truth in all of those perceptions of public relations. It does influence people, and it does utilize publicity as one of its tools. The public relations practitioner does act, on occasion, as a press agent, and he or she is frequently well dressed and articulate, with many friends and acquaintances.   ·

A more balanced view of public relations professionals is as communications specialists who seek out, utilize, and maintain communication between organizations (profit and nonprofit) and the public.

A recent paper defined the function of the public relations practitioner as a:

distinctive management function which helps establish and maintain mutual lines of communication, understanding and cooperation between an organization and its publics; involves the management of problems or issues; helps management to keep informed on and responsive to public opinion; defines and emphasizes the responsibility of management to serve the public interest; helps management to keep abreast of and effectively utilize change, serving as an early warning system to help anticipate trends; and uses research and sound ethical communication techniques as its principal tools.

Public relations jobs include:

- Writing, editing, and doing photography and layout for a monthly newsletter
- Designing and preparing audiovisual presentations
- Conceptualizing, designing, and constructing brochures and booklets used in sales and public relations programs
- Maintaining liaison with all levels of management
- Conducting external promotion campaigns
- Planning and implementing managers' meetings
- Writing parts of the annual report
- Arranging panel discussions and seminars
- Speaking to groups
- Managing press arrangements for conventions and seminars
- Planning, coordinating, and running special events such as open houses, plant tours, dedications, conventions, meetings of stockholders and community leaders
- Corresponding with the public, e.g., consumers, educators, students, stockholders
- Supplying information to the media
- Writing speeches for corporate executives; conducting speakers bureaus for groups within and outside the community
- Preparing displays, exhibits, and slides
- Planning information messages for radio, television, newspapers, and magazines

The communications student who desires a career in public relations should be skilled in assessing audience attitudes; have the ability the recognize issues dealing with communication credibility; be skilled in persuasion, especially in writing persuasive messages to the print and electronic media; be proficient in the research, organization, and practice of writing speeches for others; be able to understand which channels of communication will be most effective in the presentation of a particular message, by a particular speaker, at a particular time; and know how to receive and interpret feedback from various groups.

Most communications graduates have at least a basic understanding of public speaking, persuasion, interpersonal communication, the mass media, writing, audience research, and broadcast journalism. These areas represent core subjects from the communications discipline that have direct application to public relations.

Business and Corporate Media

It should be apparent from other sections of this book that the media—broadcast, cablecast, and print—are pervasive in the information society.

In years past, persons with strong technical, broadcast, and production-related training sought to utilize those skills in careers that would take them to the nation's media centers such as New York's radio and television corporate headquarters (ABC, NBC, CBS) or Hollywood's movie and television studios. Currently, however, colleges and universities are informing these media students about another career option: the expanding market for media jobs in corporate settings.

Many organizations are developing corporate media and media production divisions. These departments are staffed by people who have expertise in the creation, production, financing, and distribution of media-related products such as public relations videos and films, broadcast commercials, audio tapes, promotional films and videos, and education-related media products.

A recent study reports on the development of a communications course on corporate media at Emerson College. One objective of the course is to provide the student with an idea of the purposes and uses of corporate media. Cited among the uses of media in a corporate or business environment are:

- Job training
- Educational programming
- Employee orientation
- New-product information
- Sales motivation
- Sales training
- Management communication
- Promotion and public relations
- Internal corporate news
- Teleconferencing

To prepare for a career in corporate media, communications students are advised to take courses and acquire training in radio and television, photography, photojournalism, journalistic and technical writing, media design, media management, computer technology, finance and budgeting, video electronic editing, instructional design, video and audio production, and slide-tape production.

Businesses and organizations are realizing the need for media-related material and are spending large amounts of money to acquire media-trained personnel and materials. A recent report showed that business and industry account for over half of all audiovisual purchases, compared with 29 percent for elementary, secondary, and higher education combined.

In another study, media and educational technologists from six occupational settings (business and industry, government/armed services, medical institutions, colleges/universities, elementary/secondary schools, community-junior colleges/vocational-technical schools) were queried regarding job competencies for educational and media technologists. All of the groups except the military cited basic design functions such as developing individualized instruction programs, designing or coordinating materials development for courses, writing instructional guides, developing automated presentations, producing videotapes, graphic materials, and slide presentations, and improving production quality.

Much of corporate media are produced for small-group or individualized instruction. The following is a list of audiovisual materials used by many businesses and organizations:

Photography:
• original 35mm color slides
• duplicate 35mm color slides
• color prints
• black-and-white prints

Audio materials:
• original sound recording, music (including dubs)
• original sound recording, voice
• original sound recording, final mix
• audiocassettes

Video materials:
• original in-studio or on-location production
• documentation/research
• ¾″ videocassettes
• ½″ videocassettes

Training aids:
• overhead transparencies
• charts, graphs, and other graphic materials
• displays, booths, on-road exhibits
• brochures, pamphlets, training sales aids

"Canned" presentations:
- slide-tape presentations for training
- slide-tape presentations for corporate promotion
- video training/promotion
- multi-image presentations for public relations, road shows, exhibit information, fund-raising, new-product promotion, employee orientation, tourist information, sales motivation, meeting openers and closers
- 35mm, 16mm and 8mm motion pictures

Computer-Assisted instruction:
- in-service training and employee development

A number of students at Emerson with interests in media and educational technology have utilized their skills in the profit and nonprofit corporate sector. Several students produced a videotape for the Boston Police Department to teach the officers how to use a new radio communications system. One student produced slides and photos on detecting and treating eye disease for the Massachusetts Eye and Ear Infirmary. Another student wrote and produced monthly radio features to promote travel for the Massachusetts Division of Tourism. Still others produced a slide-tape show and revised informational and promotional printed material for an internship program.

More and more organizations are using and producing corporate and business media products. Computer firms, publishing companies, manufacturing firms, banks, insurance companies, utilities, retail stores, government departments, hospitals, health-care facilities, and religious organizations are all turning to corporate media. The communications and media student is therefore in demand.

The Word Processor

We used to be told, "Learn to type; it will come in handy someday!" Today's youth is hearing a different version of that recommendation: "Learn to use the word processor!"

Word processing is basically electronic typewriting; that is, the production of letters, memos, manuscripts, and reports on a machine that uses tape, card, or most frequently a disk to store the material in a memory.

Generally, the word processor consists of a keyboard, a printer, the operating program or "brain" that controls the system, and a storage memory. Most word processing systems also have a video display terminal (VDT) that permits the operator to view the text as it is entered or edited on the keyboard.

It is often said that it is virtually impossible to live in certain areas of the United States without an automobile. The same statement may be made about the future office that lacks a word processor. The word processor allows one to produce, edit, store, and retrieve written material far more rapidly and easily than ever before.

The major purpose of the word processor is to make it possible to produce a document quickly, to make frequent changes in it, to store it on a floppy disk or some other device, and to ultimately produce a perfect hard copy of it.

Word processing software packages are available that contain a stored vocabulary of thousands of hard-to-spell words. The user can have the program go over the stored text and check the spelling.

The word processor also solves the problem of producing documents that require repetition; e.g., letters, contracts, and memos. Once the document has been stored in the system's memory, it never has to be typed again. To obtain a "hard copy" of the document, one simply inserts the tape or disk and activates the printer.

COURTESY DATA GENERAL CORPORATION

A modern word processing department.

Word processing skills are important for most employees in communications fields.

Additionally, three job titles have recently emerged for those interested in the application of word processing. The *word processing specialist* produces and edits technical and statistical material and is responsible for retrieving text and other data from computerized files.

The *word processing trainer* is in great demand, especially among the high technology firms that have already adopted word processing extensively. The word processing trainer instructs new operators in use of the equipment and introduces new ideas, uses, and innovations to already experienced users. The word processing trainer works with both staff and management in integrating the equipment throughout the organization.

The *word processing supervisor* is a manager responsible for scheduling and coordinating work flow, assisting operators in the production of documents, quality control, and the overall assessment of the production of the facility.

As word processing hardware (machinery) and software (programs) become more accessible to individuals and organizations, the demand for word processing professionals will continue to grow.

COURTESY DATA GENERAL CORPORATION

Word processing supervisors schedule and coordinate the work flow.

Training and Development

The growth of courses in business and organizational communications has provided many new and exciting career options in business and government. An examination of the job listings in the employment section of the Sunday newspaper uncovers several career opportunities such as: training specialist, training coordinator, organizational development specialist, training director, and organizational research analyst.

Training and development, sometimes referred to as industrial or employee education, is used by many organizations to provide or advance employee knowledge and skill. Some training programs are technical in nature, instructing the employees or trainees in the mechanics of producing a product or providing a service.

Frequently, training involves the development of managerial or human relations (interpersonal communication) skills for employees promoted from the production to the managerial ranks. A person who is an excellent technician, machinist, engineer, or software developer may lack competence or experience in dealing with subordinates. Since skill in managing people seems to be related to a person's own job satisfaction, many new managers are given training in executive leadership and human relations.

As new ideas or innovations are diffused more rapidly in organizations, and as personnel changes are so frequent in this highly mobile society, almost every employee from the new hire to the corporate vice president can expect to participate in some form of training during his career.

The following list describes some of the responsibilities frequently required of the training and development professional:

- *Instructor*—presents information and coordinates structured learning experiences to enhance or develop individual or team skills
- *Group facilitator*—coordinates group and team discussions to express opinions, attitudes, needs, and desires to each other and to management
- *Program designer*—develops learning and behavioral objectives and designs a training program to meet those objectives.
- *Communication specialist*—identifies and works to improve or eliminate communication problems of the organization
- *Media specialist*—produces media-related products and projects such as training films or videos, slide-tape presentations, graphics, and slides

- *Organizational research analyst*—designs questionnaires and surveys to help discover the attitudes and feelings of employees; is responsible for data collection, data analysis, and writing and production of reports
- *Writer*—prepares learning and instructional materials
- *Task analyst*—identifies tasks and activities; provides human resource support
- *Personnel representative*—is responsible for new hires, interviewing, employee benefits, and other human resource activities

A recent survey to determine the most important skills required for a training and development specialist indicated that communications and human relations skills headed the list.

The study also reported that courses in interpersonal communication, organizational communication, small-group processes, management, organizational development, and organizational/industrial psychology were especially important.

The person seeking a career in training and development should also be knowledgeable in data processing, statistics, and computer applications. Recent developments in the training field suggest strong movement toward computer-based training.

Chapter **VI**

Communications in Education

We have presented a great deal of information about the expanding world of communications and telecommunications. We have mentioned innovations and technologies such as satellite communications, personal computers, and interactive video. We have looked at electronic and printed media and at the career possibilities in business communications.

One career choice, however, has not been examined. In spite of its seeming lack of opportunity in recent years, many would argue that it is the most important career of all—teaching. Those who practice it are the people who will train leaders in communications and telecommunications: advertising directors, public relations executives, print and broadcast journalists, training coordinators, and media production coordinators.

It is also the career option that will provide the new techniques, ideas, and research that will keep the field growing and expanding well into the twenty-first century.

Over the last thirty years, the profession of teaching has provided career opportunities for students trained in the communications arts and sciences. But the effects of declining enrollment of students, budget cuts, modest beginning salaries as compared to business and industry, and strong competition for jobs have dampened interest in teaching.

While many of these "problems" still exist, there are some "bright spots" in the communications field.

Although the available college-age student pool has declined over the last few years, colleges and universities have begun attracting "non-traditional" students. Typically this student is the adult who never attended college or who left college because of employment or family pressures.

In addition, a second "birth boom" has recently been identified consisting of the children of the "baby boom" generation 1946–1954. Many of the original baby boomers had delayed having children because of professional or educational priorities. As these children progress throughout the educational system, and as the various fields of communications continue to grow in popularity, secondary schools and institutions of higher education will need qualified teachers of communications.

The demand for qualified secondary school and college and university teachers of communications will continue to grow because other options have lured communications students away from teaching. The growing number of communications-related jobs and the explosion in communications technology have enticed many. Additionally, others who are interested in teaching as a career have become "educational specialists" or "trainers" in organizations or in the corporate sector. Thus teaching vacancies will exist for those seriously interested in communications education.

Finally, the field of communications has become so popular that school systems are adding more communications classes to their programs of study. Nearly every college or university has a Department of Communications or a School of Communications. The number of courses offered is increasing every year.

Similarly, secondary school systems that have offered courses in public speaking and theater/drama are adding courses to their curricula such as radio and television, film, group discussion, advanced speech, oral interpretation, and interpersonal communication. This trend also suggests the strength and draw of the communications field.

Types of Careers in Communications Education

Persons interested in careers involving the teaching of communications have several directions. Positions are available in the secondary schools, the community or junior colleges, the four-year colleges and universities, and the graduate schools. Each of these teaching contexts offers different rewards and requires different levels of educational preparations. Each also requires different levels of commitment to scholarly writing and research.

The subject areas and categories for teaching positions in communications are numerous. A recent study attempted to identify twelve-year employment trends for speech communications graduates who were interested in teaching careers at the college or university level. Among the areas identified were:

Applied communications research
Broadcasting
Communications theory
Debate
Film
Instructional media
Intercultural communications
Interpersonal communications
Language
Mass communications
Nonverbal communications
Oral interpretation

Organizational communications
Persuasion
Communications research
Rhetoric
Small-group communications
Speech communications education
Speech communications fundamentals
Visual communications
Voice and diction

The twelve-year trends indicated that the largest movement has been toward interpersonal communications, broadcasting, mass communications, communications theory, and organizational communications. A number of specializations showed consistent upward movement in demand. These included: business and professional communication/speaking, health communications, small-group communications, research design, persuasion, nonverbal communications, and intercultural communications.

Secondary Schools. Until recently, communications instruction in the secondary school was limited to a course (usually only one) in public speaking or theater/drama. With the explosion in communications that took place during the 1970s and early 1980s, many schools significantly increased the number of course offerings. Courses in group discussion, radio and television production, interpersonal communications, debate, and radio and television performance augmented the standard courses in speech and drama.

The position described as *speech communication teacher* has been the most frequently advertised. These instructors help students to understand the principles of effective communication. They prepare students for speaking and listening situations that are frequently encountered on the job and in social situations.

Communications activities, group discussions, public speaking performances, lectures, audio and videotape exercises, and oral interpretation of literature are used to train students in effective communications.

Instructors may also teach group readings of literary works and direct a reader's theater (analysis and performance of literature and other dramatic works using oral interpretation instead of acting). They also serve as communications consultants to the faculty and the community. Some educators in communications may be specialists at working with persons who need to improve voice and articulation.

Many high schools house their communications programs in the department of English. Others are forming departments of communications that offer courses ranging from broadcasting to interpersonal communications. Many communications teachers also direct extracurricular or cocurricular activities. These include oral interpretation festivals, forensic (competitive speaking) and debate tournaments, theater productions, television and radio broadcasts, and in-house cable television shows.

Communications educators in the secondary schools are encouraged to keep up with current research and professional activities in the communications arts and sciences. A recent study indicated that a large number of speech communications teachers in the secondary schools undertake advanced work. Some 44 percent of the teachers surveyed reported graduate work in progress, 33 percent had completed master's work, and 20 percent were involved with work beyond the master's degree level. Frequently they attend conventions and workshops to keep abreast of developments in the field.

Junior and Community Colleges. The 1980s have seen tremendous growth in the community college system in the United States. As "college experience" or the "college degree" is becoming a prerequisite to many jobs, more adults are returning to college, and many of them are attending community colleges. A recent study reported that more full-time students were attending community colleges than four-year colleges and universities. In addition, many "traditional" students begin their college education at community colleges and then transfer to four-year colleges and universities.

A recent edition of a national journal, *Communication Education*, was devoted to the topic of speech communication in the community colleges. It stated:

> The function of the community college communication program is threefold: to provide, as nearly as possible, instruction and experiences closely comparable in scope and quality to that of courses at the same level offered at four-year institutions; to provide instruction and experience in basic communication competencies for students enrolled in technical and applied career programs and majors; to function as a service in response to specific requests for communication training for other disciplines within the college and for groups in the community.

Because of the large enrollment of adults in community colleges, communications instructors frequently teach courses for the division of continuing education. In addition, they present workshops on communications for the college and business communities. Professional organizations often ask them to judge community speaking contests and to speak at group functions. Instructors of communications in the community college are also requested to assist the college. Their expertise in discussion methods, problem-solving, and parliamentary procedure makes them valued members of campus governing boards and all-college committees. They also conduct surveys to determine potential courses for adults. Because of the unique nature of students at the community college, communications faculty often plan coursework to assist students who are not prepared for the challenges of college.

Communications is recognized as a skill that is required in virtually all personal and professional contexts. A recent report underscored the perceived importance of communications courses at community colleges. In a survey at Prince George's Community College (Largo, Maryland), students of diverse age groups and levels of motivation consistently reported that their speech communications class was one of the most enjoyable, profitable, and transferable of all courses taken.

If this trend continues, communications instructors should be in great demand at the community college level during the next two decades.

College and University.   The teaching of communications in colleges and universities as a career is both exciting and demanding. Today's professor of communications is more likely than not required to have a doctorate. That means having spent a minimum of four years in undergraduate study, one or two years at the master's degree level, and approximately three years obtaining the doctoral degree.

The college communications teacher is not only well equipped to teach a variety of courses in his or her area of specialization (e.g., broadcasting, cable television, programming, organizational communication, advertising and public relations, oral interpretation, interpersonal communication). He or she is also considered a research professional and is required to advance the discipline by conducting research in communications.

The research can take many shapes and forms. It may involve experiments in communications or the observation and recording of communications behaviors. Case studies and field studies are popular, as is historical/critical research, or the reconstruction of a past communications event or situation.

Whatever method is used, the college professor in communications is expected to advance knowledge about communications through research and to publish the findings in one of the many scholarly communications journals.

In colleges and universities where advanced graduate work is offered, the professor will be expected to assist graduate students with their research for master's theses or doctoral dissertations.

Preparing for a Career in Communications Education

For a career in communications at the secondary school level, persons entering the teaching profession should have at least a bachelor's degree in communications or a related field. A wide variety of courses in the communications field is advisable, as well as courses in English, creative writing, computer studies, and mass communications.

A recent study reported that 70 percent of secondary speech communication teachers surveyed taught English in addition to speech, and 20 percent taught theater. Other frequently assigned courses were journalism, mass media, and radio and television.

Some states require a teaching certificate in English with speech communication credits. Other states require forty hours of communications courses taken at the bachelor's level. All fifty states and the District of Columbia require teacher certification for teaching in secondary schools. To achieve certification, students must take certain college courses in education and successfully complete several semesters of student teaching. At present a few states require a master's degree for initial certification as a secondary public school teacher.

To teach communications at the junior or community college level, you should plan on obtaining a bachelor's degree in communications from a four-year college or university and then continuing your education at the master's degree level.

Although a master's degree is not always a prerequisite to a teaching position in the community college system, more and more institutions are requiring it. Some institutions that do hire a candidate with a B.A. or B.S. in communications require that he or she pursue the master's degree.

A strong, broad-based approach to communications study at the undergraduate level is suggested as preparation for a position in the community college system. Courses from business and organizational areas, advertising and public relations, interpersonal communications, rhetoric and public address, radio, television, journalism, film, and oral interpretation should prepare you well for graduate study. This broad-based approach will provide you with the scope and flexibility to teach many different courses.

Most colleges and universities advertise and post teaching job descriptions and notices based upon an area of specialization that they need to fill. As you pursue the Ph.D. you soon accrue enough courses in one area of communications to claim a specialization. In addition, the doctoral degree almost always requires a dissertation, a major project that is conducted in your area of specialization.

The Ph.D. typically takes three years to complete beyond the master's level. The first two years are spent taking additional coursework and preparing for comprehensive or qualifying exams. The third year is spent conducting research for the dissertation.

A particular course of study for the doctorate depends upon the area of specialization the candidate is seeking. However, a few generalizations may be made regarding courses that are "essential" for anyone desiring a career teaching communications at the college level.

Since university or college teaching usually requires research, writing, and publication, it is usually necessary to take a few courses in research methods.

The communications student preparing for a career as a college teacher is intensely involved in coursework, teaching, and research, usually at the same time. In exchange for a cash stipend, tuition remission, or a graduate fellowship, doctoral students teach several undergraduate courses in communications. Many of today's professors gained their first experience with college teaching as university teaching assistants. Doctoral students serve as apprentice instructors within the department, starting with the basic undergraduate course and progressing to more advanced teaching assignments. Doctoral study is an excellent test of your teaching and researching skills.

Communications Consulting

In the last ten years, a new career direction has opened up for many communications teachers, namely, *communications consulting*. A communications consultant offers his or her expertise to persons and organizations other than students. The following activities have been identified by several communications professors-consultants:

- Conducting workshops on group decision-making, listening, or presentational speaking for police officers, engineers, or corporate managers
- Serving as a facilitator for primary and secondary school teachers designing a communications curriculum
- Writing speeches and coaching corporate executives on the effective presentation of that speech

- Designing a workshop and a set of exercises on persuasion and attitude change for a corporate manager to present to his sales staff
- Training police chiefs on how to present themselves effectively when they are approached by the media
- Serving as an idea generator and critic for corporate communications officers
- Designing and conducting an attitude survey on employee benefits and employer-employee communications for a large health-care organization
- Conducting a "team-building" workshop for a group of managers in a high-technology computer firm
- Training local television reporters and personalities on how to present themselves more effectively

One common feature is apparent in the list: The communications consultant applies theory, research, and teaching to nonacademic situations.

Several recommendations are offered to communications students interested in branching off from academic teaching into careers in communications consulting. First, continue your education beyond the bachelor's degree level.

Second, enroll in many graduate courses in communications.

Third, acquire internship experience. For instance, spend the summer as an intern doing research and report writing for a high-tech computer firm. One student was employed as an intern in a large health maintenance organization, being responsible for employee benefits and career development research. After completion of her summer internship, she was called in several times by the HMO as a paid consultant researching and writing personnel-related reports.

Assess your personal qualities and interpersonal style to see if they can adjust to the rigors and time demands of paid communications consulting. You must feel comfortable working under the pressures of deadlines and time constraints. Consultants often do not have the luxury of weeks of preparation, analysis, and feedback. Reports may have to be written within a day or two of data-gathering.

Finally, make sure that your own communications style can be adapted to the nonacademic setting. Try to appear competent without being condescending. Learn to defer to the client's expertise, to communicate persuasively, and to exercise practicality.

Resources, Associations, and Placement Services

The teaching profession mandates that its members actively participate in professional associations and organizations. The communications field is constantly changing and innovating. New ideas, new teaching techniques, and new requirements are being adopted and diffused. Consequently it is in the best interests of the communications educator to join and participate in professional organizations. A partial listing of the many associations available to those interested in teaching is given in Appendix A.

Chapter VII

Preparing for a Communications Career

As in any profession, knowledge and skills are requisite for getting your first job. Where to study and what to study are major considerations. But before making final decisions, you ought to keep three goals clearly and constantly in mind:

- First, you need an education that, by design and curriculum, improves and perfects your communications skills.
- Second, you need an education that broadens your understanding of communications and telecommunications.
- Third, you need an education that contributes to your general knowledge.

Although it is best to balance all three goals, some educational institutions tend to emphasize certain areas over others. It is also possible that you, by your course selection, may do the same. Try to avoid repeating what you already know. New courses and information are needed. You should not take the easy routes.

It is clear from looking at the job listings of the Sunday newspaper in your city or town that at a minimum a bachelor's degree is a prerequisite for many jobs and careers in communications and related fields.

Surely there are success stories among those who did not attend college, but in comparison to those who did, they are few. The statistical probability of success is firmly on the side of the college graduate. More jobs are open to male and female graduates, and their average annual incomes are higher.

Many jobs stipulate a college degree as a requirement. This is always true in teaching, and it is almost always the case in higher-level government jobs. In a booklet entitled *Careers in Television*, the National Association of Broadcasters states:

Thus those who want to make a career in broadcasting, and to give themselves the best chance to progress to the top ranks in the industry, should carefully consider the value of college training which will give them broader vision, a depth of understanding, and skill in learning new concepts rapidly. Television is competitive and is likely to become more so, and the college-trained individual has a marked advantage both in finding a job and in advancing in the industry. In the future, college training will probably be more important because of the rise of professionalism in the industry.

In a first-time experience away from home (or, if you are a commuter, a new experience in a new environment), you will see things that went unnoticed before. Each new term, course, professor, student event, and friend will present new communications opportunities. The years in college will enhance your chances to define your direction, get some basic experience, meet future professional colleagues, make valuable contacts, and get a chance to think about issues that confront individuals and society at large that you may never again have the opportunity (or the time) to think about.

Rarely can college be considered a "lost" experience; nevertheless, you will want to get the most from it. The following are important questions.

Selecting an Institution

What type of institution? First, you should pursue the bachelor's degree, but that does not mean that the completion of the degree need take place under one roof, at one institution. Many persons prefer studying at one college for four years; the advantages of this approach are numerous, especially if the college has a strong communications program. However, there is nothing wrong with transferring if it is done with clear academic objectives—not merely for a change of scenery. Some community or junior colleges offer excellent communications courses, along with some fine equipment, and thus give you an excellent "jumping-off" point into a four-year institution. In any case, communications skills are not learned instantly; they take time to develop. Thus a degree program is usually the best avenue for most students.

Certain colleges feature certain types of bachelor's programs, the best known of which is the traditional liberal arts curriculum: majors in the humanities, social sciences, and sciences. Many of the smaller and middle-sized "liberal arts colleges" provide excellent programs with very high standards. Such a curriculum can be a strong basis for a communications career.

The more traditional liberal arts colleges, however, do not usually offer much in the way of "professional training" for a given career. Thus, although you may acquire a great deal of knowledge, you may not have the opportunity to learn some rudimentary things about your profession. The strength of your liberal arts background, however, may give you an edge in other respects.

Think twice, however, about enrolling in a liberal arts college whose reputation matches its smallness in size—*if* you are interested in communications as a profession. The result may be that you will not have been exposed to the rigors of high standards, nor will you have received the essential "professional training." Four years may have left you better educated, perhaps, but with little background in your field.

Most schools provide a combination of approaches: a liberal arts background with specialized or professional majors. Their diversity will offer you many choices and a wide variety of experiences. If designed properly, certain combinations of courses, or programs, can provide you with optimum preparation for communications. The person who is interested in news reporting, for example, might be able to choose from a wide assortment of courses in English, journalism, history, political science, government, and communications. Usually the largest and most prestigious state universities offer excellence in all areas. But you need to be cautious of universities that appear to offer much variety but in doing so sacrifice depth in certain areas, or universities so rigid in their requirements that they allow for little flexibility in the selection of elective courses.

There are also a number of communications colleges or schools, many of which are affiliated with a university. Their instructional budgets are spent in the specialized areas, and their curricula are designed to provide depth and scope. With many options built into the programs, they provide an excellent approach to learning one's field. Emerson College in Boston is one such institution at which the program is built around the communications discipline. Others include the School of Public Communications at Boston University, the S. I. Newhouse School of Public Communication at Syracuse University, the College of Communications at the University of Illinois, the School of Speech at Northwestern University, the College of Communications at the University of Texas at Austin, and the School of Interpersonal Communication at Ohio University.

Whether you are in a liberal arts, diverse, or specialized college, you ought to seek out a program that allows you to "totally immerse" yourself in your chosen profession for at least one full year. This should normally occur in the senior year when, after having taken several courses in your specialization in the freshman through junior years, you can devote your full energies to communications. Advanced courses, seminars, and work-study internships should all be part of your curriculum. If you have attended a liberal arts or nonspecialized institution, you might consider a one- or two-year master's program, which gives you the chance for full-time specialization.

What location? We have said that a communications worker ought to enjoy cities—the people, the arts, and the activities. So it isn't bad thinking to consider among your first choices colleges and universities in or near urban centers.

For one thing, urban colleges have the advantage of drawing upon the professional resources of the city to supplement the curriculum. Well-known professionals and communications personalities and scholars are available for lectures. Broadcasting stations, newspapers, theaters, advertising firms, and communications production houses are usually available for scheduled lecture tours. Businesses and organizations are plentiful in urban areas, with increasing demand for student interns. Part-time jobs and internships can be found, and such jobs often open the door to greater opportunities.

Most important, there are many chances to integrate yourself into the world of communications. The people whom you meet will provide job leads for you. The tales of individuals who have swept floors in television stations and risen to success are based partly on fact. The nearness of the profession to your college will, in itself, give you the confidence and encouragement to make your first contacts.

The activities and pace of city life are factors that prepare the communications professional for his most difficult task—that of "staying ahead." You will need to know and stay with the mood of the times. The city provides the most contemporary environment.

Surely there are disadvantages to city life: the expense, the noise, the crowding. Sometimes you will hardly have the time to create and think. Many of the larger state universities, although situated in small towns, do offer an urbanlike atmosphere. The activities are constant—shows, lectures, music, and social events. Communications opportunities are numerous.

While the urban campus provides contact with the arts and with business and organizations, and the small campus provides tranquility, you must exercise caution before enrolling in a small college far removed from an urban center. The communication arts and sciences almost mandate some available contact with the media and business.

If it is your choice not to "take on" the city when you go to college, and you have found the right college near your home, consider at least the possibility of spending a semester or two—or perhaps your master's program—near an urban location.

What size institution? There is, of course, no cut-and-dried formula about the size of an institution that might be best for your needs. But communications skills need a lot of development and much personal attention. An impersonal college is not what you want. Much will depend upon the attitude of professors rather than the size of the institution. The larger universities will present you with a lot of competition when it comes to auditioning for the campus radio station or getting on the staff of the college newspaper. Although competition of this sort is healthy, the college should not exclude you from these important experiences. If it does, look elsewhere.

What facilities? The authors have seen some excellent, but unused, facilities at colleges where there is little student or faculty interest. Other colleges with poorer facilities are overtaxed by constant usage and breakdowns. In other words, you should appraise the quality of the education before you look at the equipment.

A college that specializes in television production should have relatively up-to-date hardware and studio facilities. A budgetary problem is no excuse. It is essential that you learn on the proper equipment and in the best facilities. The larger state universities generally have the best equipment, but your decision will be based mostly on which skills you wish to obtain. Many communications areas do not require the use of technical equipment. Evaluate and choose the institution according to your specific goal.

What curriculum does the institution have? An institution should be selected according to how many relevant subject areas it can provide for you. But no college will have everything you want. Or if it does, the courses may not be offered at convenient times. You should be able to make some general observations about the curriculum by answering some very basic questions:

- Does the college have a major in communications? Some institutions say that you can specialize in communications but offer only the most basic courses. Students have had to uproot and transfer to other institutions to get the proper training.
- Examine the size of the faculty in all areas of communications. Are there as many faculty members as there are in other areas— for example, in history or economics? If not, it might indicate something about the commitment of the college to communications or the popularity of the department. On the other hand, some very small communications departments are excellent. In that case, you will have to judge from what you have heard of its reputation.
- Variety and depth are important factors in preparing yourself for

communications. Compare catalogs and make sure that there are many courses in your chosen field.

A Basic Guide to Colleges

Listed in Appendix II are colleges that offer speech and communications courses and curricula. Many of the institutions have graduate programs, which, incidentally, is a good way of judging the depth of the school's curriculum. The list is selective and by no means comprehensive, but it does provide a starting point.

What You Must Know

The selection of a college presents some interesting and exciting choices, but learning the things pertinent to your profession will be a task of a different sort.

Most community colleges, colleges, and graduate schools provide an adviser. With that person, you may discuss your objectives and determine the best course of study. If you have chosen the right institution, it will have a large variety of courses, and that is where the advice you receive will count most. No two persons have the same goals. Thus, it is very important to choose the combination of courses that will best suit you.

Because the communications field is so broad and diverse, study in any given area can prove profitable. A course in anything from auto mechanics to history might provide you with the information and background that, combined with your communications skills, would lead you into a communications career in that profession. In other words, nothing is irrelevant. Your first objective, therefore, is to educate yourself in the areas of the communications field that interest you.

Seeing things from a communications point of view, however, and getting the right skills requires an educational design of some sort. The following pages will provide some basic and fundamental guidance. But before considering specific subject areas, you should be prepared to see things from three points of view: (1) liberal arts background; (2) areas of specialization and majors; and (3) areas of complementary subject matter often called minors.

Liberal Arts

Liberal arts subject areas offer you factual knowledge, stimulating ideas, and an opportunity to express your own opinions. If the last ingredient is missing, you will not be improving upon your communications abilities.

Liberal arts subjects are frequently theoretical. They are not taught in such a way as to provide you with specific techniques for specific jobs. Indirect as they are, the things you learn from the liberal arts are essential for a communications career. Many successful persons currently working in communications began their formal education by getting a foundation in the liberal arts and then pursuing an advanced degree or additional courses in communications. The liberal arts offerings provide a breadth of knowledge, research abilities, mental discipline, and open-mindedness.

Among the countless liberal arts courses, it is advantageous to take those that *reinforce* your interests and direction in communications. Ten typical and useful liberal arts course areas are:

- Psychology
- Computer applications
- Statistics
- Introduction to sociology
- Writing and composition
- Economics
- History
- Introduction to the visual arts
- English
- Drama and visual imagination
- Political science

Each area will reinforce your education while opening up new ideas and areas for investigation.

Specialization and the Communications Major

According to most guidance counselors, you should select a major that will provide you with (1) a general knowledge of the field and the optional directions within it, and (2) the special skills that are directly applicable to your professional direction. A solid major is both theoretical and practical. While many young scholars question the need to study materials that are theoretical, the established practitioner will readily admit that it is theory that guides effective practice. The famous social psychologist Kurt Lewin frequently has said, "There is nothing so practical as a good theory." Concepts and ideas along with skill development should be balanced. One should not be sacrificed for the other.

Some institutions like to offer a multifaceted approach to your major in communications. These institutions provide the student with competence in oral communications skills, communications theory and research, and training in the application of communications principles to various communications situations, e.g., public relations, advertising, personnel, teaching, counseling, and media.

It is true that many communications professionals have come from varied areas and disciplines. But in the past twenty years or so very few colleges had many courses in the communications area. People usually learned about the field by engaging in extracurricular activities such as the campus newspaper, the college radio station, and speech contests. In the last ten years, however, society's recognition of the importance of communications has created thousands of new departments and courses throughout the country and the world. Such departments include: communications studies, journalism, radio and television, computer studies, speech, communication disorders, telecommunications, mass communications, and many others. High schools are still somewhat behind, but most offer such basic areas as speech, drama, journalism, radio, and debate.

Complementary Minors

Minor areas—that is, those areas that require less specialization and fewer courses—can be of vital importance to the communications professional. The field's adaptability to other areas makes it important to have specializations that complement—or broaden—your abilities. An international correspondent, for example, would find history, government, political science, and international affairs to be excellent minors for his major in mass communications, radio and television, or journalism. A director of training and development for an organization would find that business, business administration, computer science, or industrial or social psychology would make excellent choices for minor areas of study.

It is possible to reverse this process, making international affairs your major and mass communications your minor. The depth you would acquire in international affairs might be excellent, but it might minimize your chances of getting your first job in communications because fewer options would be open to you. A major in communications will provide more job options in production, advertising, announcing, training and development, public relations, and mediation.

Suggested Majors and Minors for Communications Careers

As mentioned before, it is not to your advantage to classify yourself into one job specialization once and for all. Flexibility is all-important. The majors and minors listed below, as well as the job categories, are intended for guidance only. The titles of majors and minors vary from institution to institution.

SAMPLE MAJORS AND MINORS FOR COMMUNICATIONS CAREERS

Communications Profession	*Possible Majors or Minors*
Communications and Education	Speech and Communications Studies, or Communications Mass Communications or Journalism Speech Pathology and Audiology or Communication Disorders Education Computer Studies or Sciences
Advertising and Marketing	Business, Advertising, or Marketing Business and Organizational Communications Speech Communications Mass Communications, Radio and Television Journalism, English, or Creative Writing Psychology, Sociology and Social Science Computer Science Art and Design
Broadcasting	Mass Communications, Radio and Television, Broadcasting Speech and Communications Studies Business Communications Film Journalism or Creative Writing Theater and Dramatic Arts Advertising, Marketing, or Public Relations Commercial Art
Writing and Publishing	English or Journalism Creative Writing and Publishing Technical Writing Speech Communications

Communications Profession	*Possible Majors or Minors*
	Business and Organizational Communications
	Mass Communications
Educational and/or Corporate Media	Educational and Corporate Media
	Mass Communications
	Film and Video
	Education
	Business Communications
	Communications Studies or Speech
	Journalism and Creative and Professional/Technical Writing
	Psychology, Industrial Psychology, Sociology, and the Social Sciences
	Theater and Dramatic Arts
	Art, Commercial Art, Graphics
	Public Relations
	Advertising
Sales and/or Business Communications	Business and Organizational Communications
	Business Administration
	Advertising and Marketing
	Public Relations
	Management and Industrial Psychology
	Computer Science
	Speech and Communications Studies
	Interpersonal Communications
	Sociology and the Social Sciences
Training and Development	Communications Studies
	Education
	Industrial and Social Psychology
	Business and Organizational Communications
	Theater and Dramatic Arts
	Mass Communications
	Professional and Creative Writing
	Technical Writing
	Film and Video
Personnel	Education, Guidance, and Counseling
	Psychology, Sociology and Social Sciences
	Industrial Psychology
	Speech and Communications Studies
	Interpersonal Communications
	Business and Organizational Communications

Communications Profession	Possible Majors or Minors
Public Relations	Business Administration, Public Relations, Advertising, or Marketing Business and Organizational Communications Mass Communications Journalism Creative and Professional Writing English Psychology, Sociology and Social Sciences
International Communications	International Studies, Intercultural Communications, International Communications, World History, Diplomatic History Speech and Communications Studies Interpersonal Communications Languages Mass Communications Public Relations, Business, Organizational Communications
Politics and Legal Services	Speech and Communications Studies Political Science Business Administration or Law English and Creative Writing Interpersonal Communications Psychology, Sociology and the Social and Behavioral Sciences Communications and Persuasion
Government and Social Services	Political Science Communications Studies Government Social Work Urban Studies Public Administration Journalism Mass Media and Communications Public Relations Speech Pathology and Audiology, or Communication Disorders International Affairs History

Specific Subjects

Not too many years ago, the liberal arts curriculum dominated most of higher education. A solid basis in the humanities, social sciences, and sciences was considered the best general preparation for many fields. This educational approach is still very sound and is used at many colleges and universities.

Some of the subject areas listed throughout this chapter have been and still are part of many liberal arts curricula. "Liberal arts" is, after all, a very broad term and includes the "Communications Arts and Sciences." This is a description of all subjects—whether they be in the professional area of communications or in the liberal arts—that teach the skills, talents, and information pertinent to the field. A course in a sociology department called Group Behavior may have some aspects of communications that directly apply to your career objectives. The same is true for courses in other departments such as Computer Applications, Industrial Psychology, Educational Technology, and Business Law. These courses could be listed under your heading of communications arts and sciences.

This approach of picking and choosing courses from all areas that have the most direct relationship to your career is often called "interdisciplinary education." Some colleges offer interdisciplinary majors, but in most instances you achieve the same results by selecting the right combination of courses. An adviser who knows and understands your career objectives will be able to help you.

The titles of courses vary so widely from school to school that it is best to think of what you need in terms of "subject areas" rather than courses. A glance at the college catalog will reveal if a particular course covers your needed areas. The most essential areas are included in the following pages.

Communications Skills

We have spoken often about the need for communications skills because they are critical to your profession. Without skills in communications you will not go far in any profession or occupation. Even if your direct role is not that of communicator (as we defined it earlier), you will be using communications skills in your everyday work—to make contact with people, to issue directions, to present ideas, in interview situations, in meetings, to write letters, or to carry on all of the day-to-day activities of your profession.

Place communications skills, therefore, at the center of your curriculum. By doing so, you will be able to relate all other subject areas to your skills, and vice versa. Then you will be able to move out, from your core of communication skills, into many professional or academic areas. Consider this diagram.

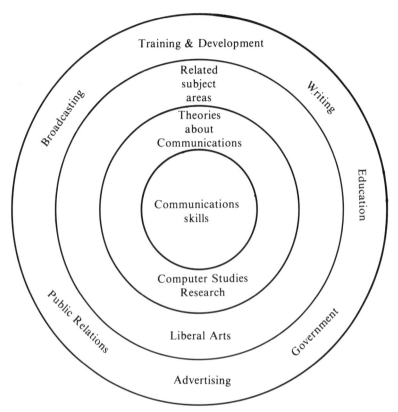

Courses in communications skills ought to offer you exposure to and training in the following areas:

1. The *language* of speaking and writing. Conciseness, clarity, vocabulary, grammar, word choice, emphasis, factors of interest, vitality—all the elements of effective language style.
2. The *organization* of speaking and writing. All aspects of outlining, putting ideas together, logical structure, development, unity, coherence, and emphasis.

3. The *types* of speaking and writing. Styles necessary for adapting to different audiences and media. Some types include: informative, persuasive, entertaining, argumentative, and creative. They include short forms of communication such as commercials, interviews, and long forms such as essays and speeches, as well as discussion, editorializing, factual description, and fictional description.

4. The *presentational methods* of communications. These include mostly elements of performance such as volume and voice projection, articulation, voice variety, nonverbal aspects such as gestures and facial expression, body movement, interpreting, acting, reading, announcing, oral communication expression, and presentation of technical information.

5. The *listening and observational abilities* of communications. Includes skills of listening, feedback, comprehending, and remembering information, or observing news, events, actions, behavior, and any other details involved in communications.

6. The *human relations* or *interpersonal communications* skills. These include the skills necessary to interact effectively with people in managerial contexts. Important skills in this area include the ability to express confidence and to be decisive, to give others performance feedback, to give clear directions, to be sensitive to the needs of others with whom you come in contact in the day-to-day and work environment.

Analytical Abilities

The art of effective communications also involves an understanding of how, why, and when communication takes place. Whether you are a communicator, an analyst, a producer, or a technician, you will need to know the theories and information of the field. Your courses ought to include fundamental information about the following:

1. An understanding of *human behavior.* This includes psychology and educational psychology (important for teaching and educational media), sociology, organizational behavior, interpersonal communication, social psychology, industrial psychology, sociology, political sociology, urban studies, cultural and physical anthropology, intercultural communication, communication theory, understanding of consumer behavior (motives and reasons for buying), sex, and public tastes.

2. An understanding of *logic and the reasoning processes.* Involves

subject areas such as argumentation, tests of evidence, logic, philosophy, problem-solving, and conference planning. Could also involve dramatic structure, literary structure, and all forms of organization.

3. An understanding of *communication processes*. This requires a knowledge of *how* (through what systems and methods) communication takes place. Subject areas are communications theory; the study of communication between persons, groups, organizations, cultures, and races; language and language difficulties; semantics; and nonverbal communication, the approaches to studying communications.

4. An understanding of *communications research*. Includes marketing research, questioning and interviewing, conducting research in organizations, polling techniques, statistics, tests, population stratification. Includes also the design and running of experimental studies in communications, psychology, and sociology.

5. An understanding of *computer science and computer applications*. Designed to provide the student with a general knowledge of the concepts and use of computers as tools for data storage and manipulation at home, on the job, and for communications research.

6. *General knowledge*. Knowledge of all things can serve to enrich your understanding and appreciation as well as providing the facts necessary for communications. Includes history, economics, national issues, literature, fine arts, ecology, science, drama—anything!

The Production of Communications

Skills and analytical abilities are a must for a future in communications. But your knowledge of the production of communications may be limited, or extensive, depending upon which direction you choose to take. Some general knowledge of the fundamentals of production are useful to all communications professionals, however.

1. A knowledge of *administration*. Includes media management, television production, television directing, station administration, directing, advertising production, business communications, corporate media, educational administration, public administration, and all administrative areas.

2. A knowledge of the different *communications formats and media*. Variety of subject areas includes the production of all

written forms—from pamphlets to books, advertising layout, programmed instruction, multimedia systems, video and film production, broadcasting production, camera mechanics, sound recording techniques, videotape editing, set editing, computer graphics.

3. A knowledge of the *materials and processes needed for production.* A background of information and facts, or at least a knowledge of where to find such information, is needed concerning the uses of equipment, special effects, lighting materials, background music, video and film clips, and a wide assortment of production materials.

4. A knowledge of the *costs of production.* Includes budgeting, accounting, the costs of communications equipment, the costs of talent, the costs of lighting and all other materials, financial management.

The Technology of Communications

From a cassette tape recorder to a highly complex television system, skills in operating equipment or developing communications materials are very useful. Such skills involve something more than a knowledge *about* technology; they include the actual making, producing, and operations.

Technical information about such equipment can be extremely complex. Thus, if one is interested in the design or manufacture of it, a career in electrical engineering would be a better route to take.

The communications technologist, however, is more interested in how materials can be used to produce *an effect.* What types of print, or colors, should be used in an advertisement? How do you get the best mood, or effect, out of a photograph of a product? These are questions that the media technologist is capable of answering with comprehensive knowledge of materials. To that end, any course in visuals, graphics, broadcasting operations, lighting—or whatever—is useful.

Is Too Much Expected of You?

We have covered much ground, and we have suggested that you learn many things. It wouldn't be unnatural if you asked, "Is the field of communications too broad? Am I asked to know too much? Will I be expected to know more than I can handle?"

We do not think so. Even though the process of developing your communications skills is a lifetime project, you probably have obtained a good head start without really knowing it. Your elementary and secondary education should have given you the basics of speaking and writing. And if your interest is strong, you can overcome your major problems. Chances are that you may already have started an activity or a hobby that will aid you in your development.

Extracurricular activities are, in fact, a good way of testing yourself. You can discover whether your interest is strong, or whether you have a talent, or whether you want to continue your study in a college major or in the courses we have described. Most important, extracurricular activity can help prepare you for the direction ahead.

Most of these activities will be available in your own school or community. If not, start one.

Some popular communications activities include:

The school newspaper	Journalism club
The debate team	Essay contests
Speaking contests	Radio station
Computer clubs	Videotaping
Extemporaneous speaking contests	Audiovisual assistance
Oral interpretation festivals or contests	Language club
	Photography club
Variety shows	Sports announcing and reporting
Class plays	Art contests
Film and animation clubs	
Comedy workshops	

If you still fear that too much might be expected of you, you should keep in mind that whatever you learn in communications usually has many purposes and can be applied in many directions. Because each area reinforces your communications abilities in other areas, your development can take place easily if you recognize these relationships. These qualities involve simply:

DOING—Communication skills
THINKING—Analytical abilities
DEVELOPING—The production of communications
MAKING OR OPERATING—The technology of communications

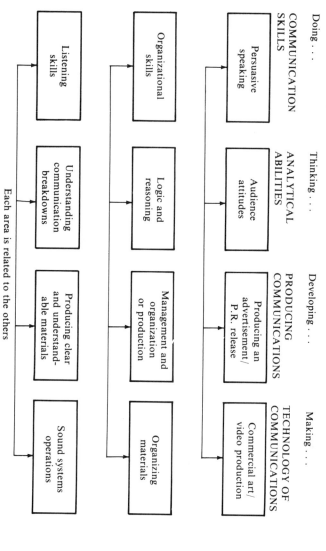

COMPLEMENTARY SKILLS IN COMMUNICATIONS

Doing . . .
Thinking . . .
Developing . . .
Making . . .

COMMUNICATION SKILLS
ANALYTICAL ABILITIES
PRODUCING COMMUNICATIONS
TECHNOLOGY OF COMMUNICATIONS

Persuasive speaking
Audience attitudes
Producing an advertisement/ P.R. release
Commercial art/ video production

Organizational skills
Logic and reasoning
Management and organization or production
Organizing materials

Listening skills
Understanding communication breakdowns
Producing clear and understand-able materials
Sound systems operations

Each area is related to the others

Chapter VIII

The Job Search

Sooner or later, you will be faced with the trickiest task of all—landing a job. But if you have acquired the right education and some experience in the real world, your objectives should be quite clear. You will know what type of job you want; you will have an idea of your talents and abilities. Nothing creates confidence more than a good sense of how your talents match up with the requirements of specific jobs. If you are uncertain as to what you are qualified to do, it is time for another survey of your abilities and interests. But let's assume you are certain, and you are ready to proceed.

There is always that first step, however. Your first job may be only an introduction or training ground for what you ultimately want. Thus, you need to ask yourself some preliminary questions.

Setting Your First Professional Objectives

What type of position are you looking for? There are, of course, many levels of job opportunities in any field. You would rather not start at the broom-pushing level. Yet, the long-range advantages of being employed by an important company may mean that you accept a not-so-fancy job title. Beware, however, of underrating yourself just for the sake of obtaining a job with a prestigious company or media firm. The lower you start, the longer it will take to advance. Moreover, you will be wasting valuable time that could have been spent learning important skills for your next step.

Many jobs can fall into the "dead-end" category. A receptionist's position at a large corporation may make you feel important, but it may get you nowhere. Your talents will be used for nothing more than saying "hello" with a smile.

The wise course, therefore, is to set a job range that is neither too high nor too low for your abilities. This can be done by searching for, and categorizing, jobs that are easy, jobs that are moderately challenging, and jobs that are very challenging. From these groupings, you will be able to make your final choice according to what seems to offer the best future.

What salary level? Some of the same type of considerations apply to this question. Are you willing to sacrifice salary for prestige? Are you willing to sacrifice salary for certain kinds of experience? Are you willing to sacrifice salary for location? Or are you willing to sacrifice salary at all?

It is self-defeating to accept less than what you are worth, especially if it becomes a pattern. The talents necessary for communications professions are often difficult to judge in terms of financial value, so it is easy to rate yourself too high or too low. Most persons tend to underrate themselves.

Some financial flexibility might be necessary for your first job. After all, you do need that first full-time experience. Thus, you may have to sacrifice something. But if it means accepting slave wages, forget it. There will be a future for you if you are able and persistent. So look elsewhere. Jobs that pay too poorly will get you nowhere.

What location? Many communications professionals recommend that you start, if possible, in an urban location. More experience, more contacts, and more information are available in the big city. If your choice is between an urban area that has a high cost of living and a nonurban area that does not, you still are likely to find more advantages in the urban area. The availability of free-lance work, for example, will possibly replace the financial loss.

Densely populated areas have the greatest need for communications. And where there is more competition in the field is the place where you are likely to acquire the sharpest and most professional skills.

What experience will you get? High salary or low? Urban or rural location? Important as these questions are, they are not as important as the most vital question of all: What experience will you get? The radio station that gives you the most intense, most varied, and best training is the most desirable place of employment.

A job in a large organization confines you to small tasks. But at a smaller company, an advertising agency for example, you may be doing everything—account executive work, production work, writing, selling, dining with clients, and making contacts with the media.

Using Professional and Academic Placement Associations

In your next step, you will need to consider what sources you will turn to for finding positions. The first, and most obvious, answer is your professional or academic placement association.

The advantage of going through an association, whose purpose it is to bring together its members for conventions and to publish information of interest to all, is that it is neutral. Unlike an employment agency, it has nothing to gain or lose by placing you. It simply provides job information. There is no pressure, and the option of making the job contact is totally your own.

Professional associations, such as the Speech Communication Association, have placement services that are reasonably priced. Membership in the association is necessary, however, before you join the placement service. Academic nonprofit associations of this sort have high ethical standards, and so you can trust job descriptions to be honest. Your credentials will be handled with the utmost confidence.

Another major advantage of the professional association is that its job descriptions come from all parts of the country, and sometimes of the world. Because there are no geographical limitations, you will have more choices. Moreover, such a broad picture of the employment possibilities in your profession can alert you to what salary levels are realistic for a person with your qualifications. As a permanent member of the association, you will also have access to information about the trends of employment. You are, therefore, staying on top of the job market and thereby providing yourself with more job mobility should the opportunities arise.

Professional and academic placement services are usually operated through the mail and at conventions. Attendance at conventions will give the opportunity to meet many prospective employers in a short time. Printed materials in the form of pamphlets and reports provide addresses of people to write to concerning employment. Even a conversation in the convention hotel's elevator may lead to an outstanding job opportunity.

One disadvantage of the professional association placement service is that it usually limits you to one type of profession in your field, such as teaching. Journalism associations list journalism positions, and broadcasting associations list broadcasting positions. You should, therefore, look to other sources of information for different types of job opportunities. An extensive list of professional associations is given in Appendix I.

Many schools and colleges have placement offices that will aid you, at little cost, in finding jobs. An assortment of occupational literature is usually available at no cost. These offices will keep your records and recommendations on file and send them out at your request.

Employment Agencies

An acceptable and sometimes excellent way of making job contacts is through employment agencies. Agencies operate for a profit, which they obtain by charging a service fee either to the job applicant or to the employer. They are interested, therefore, in bringing together applicants and employers who are satisfied with one another.

Some agencies have reputations for aggressive placement with little concern for the job seeker's real needs. But this need not frighten you away from agencies. Most are reputable. A thorough and ethical agency will interview you, find out your long-range goals, examine your qualifications, and talk with you honestly about your chances for employment and the salary you can expect to receive.

You should, however, understand thoroughly the fee requirements and contractual arrangements of the agency. Some firms charge you the employment fee. If you lose a job through no fault of your own, you should not be charged the fee. If you resign or are fired for a fault of your own, then your fee will not be refunded. In instances where you decide not to accept the job obtained for you, you may have to pay the fee—depending on the contract. Often the fee is paid by your employer. But if you accept the job and fail to show up for work, you may be required to pay the fee.

The main advantage of agencies is that they profit by your success. That factor alone motivates them to find you a job. Good agencies will look at your résumé and figure out ways of emphasizing your particular talents to an employer. They may also discuss the appropriate things to say in your interview. You may find out some things about yourself you did not previously know.

There are some disadvantages as well. The fee is one—if you have to pay it. Second, very few agencies specialize in communications positions. Such positions are promoted in the trade, through journals, by word of mouth, and in classified advertisements. Thus, agency listings in your specialty may be quite limited.

Classified Advertisements

The process of going through many advertisements and writing to many companies can be long and tedious. Many of your letters will bring no responses. After much investigation, many mailings, and a lot of waiting, you still may not have a job you want.

But classified advertisements do provide one of the best sources of information. Do not limit yourself to one newspaper, however. Check your local library for newspapers from other cities. It is important, also, not to limit yourself to looking at advertisements that describe one specific job title, such as "Public Relations Director." Certainly such jobs are available, but the skills of the public-relations worker are sometimes listed under different job titles.

PUBLICATION EDITOR

A specialist in Business Communication is what we're after!

This position offers editorial responsibility for a technically-oriented publication. THE HARTFORD AGENT, one of our principal means of communication to agents representing The Hartford Group.

Since this individual will be charged with the complete development of this publication, those we consider should have a degree in English or Journalism, with some experience covering all facets of publishing — i.e., art, photography, layout, production know-how and budget management.

Communicate!

Express Yourself!

Communication Positions

Writing a Résumé

Before applying for a job, you will need to write a résumé. The résumé is your fact sheet; it is a summary of who you are and what you do. Upon looking at it, your prospective employer will make some preliminary judgments about your qualifications.

For this reason, and because you are in communications, *your résumé must be perfect.* It cannot have any spelling errors, erasures, or imperfections of any sort. It is an advertisement for yourself, and as such it should receive a great deal of attention from you. You must go over it—twenty-five times if necessary—to make sure it is accurate, well designed, and letter-perfect.

What Is a Résumé?

A well-written résumé is an important component of your job search. Its purpose is to present your qualifications clearly to prospective employers. Coupled with an individualized cover letter, an employer can quickly assess your potential value to his/her organization. While a résumé rarely gets you a job, it can entice an employer into offering you an interview. Therefore, it needs to be clear, concise, and written with the employer's needs in mind.

Preparation

Whether you're writing your résumé for the first time or updating it for the twentieth time, it can be an overwhelming experience. Thoughtful preparation can help to ease the anxiety. Begin by assessing your technical and personal qualifications. Next, consider specific types of employers with whom you are interested in working and the employee qualifications they are seeking. Then write a résumé that describes your qualifications in terms of an employer's needs.

Résumé Format

Although there is no "right" résumé format, it is important to choose one that best describes your qualifications. Remember, your main objective in writing the résumé is to get an interview. With that in mind, consider the following formats and think about which one will best convey your accomplishments to a prospective employer.

The Chronological Résumé. This has been the most widely used and accepted format in the past. Jobs are listed in reverse chronological order (most recent job first). Dates of employment are usually listed first, followed by the name of the organization, and then job title.

Advantages of a chronological résumé:

• Professional interviewers are familiar with it
• It is the easiest to prepare, since its content is structured by employment dates, companies, and titles
• It can show a steady employment record and possible upward progression in job responsibility
• It provides the interviewer with a guide for discussing work experience

Disadvantages of a chronological résumé:

• It can reveal gaps in your employment
• It can suggest instability if you have jumped from job to job
• It may put undesired emphasis on a job area that you want to minimize

- Skills and accomplishments are difficult to see, particularly if you have little direct job experience

The Functional Résumé. This format highlights skills and qualifications with little emphasis on dates. Advantages of a functional résumé:

- It stresses specific skill areas that you want to market
- It helps camouflage a spotty employment record
- It allows you to emphasize professional growth
- You can deemphasize positions not related to your current career goal

Disadvantages of a functional résumé:

- Some employers are suspicious of it and may want to see additional work history
- Companies and organizations for whom you have worked are not highlighted

The Combination Résumé. As the name suggests, the combination résumé includes company names and dates from the chronological résumé and skills and achievements from the functional résumé. Advantages of the combination résumé:

- It provides a good opportunity to emphasize those skills that the employer needs
- Gaps in employment can be deemphasized
- It can be varied to emphasize chronology or functional skills

A distinct disadvantage of the combination résumé:

- It takes longer to read, and an employer may lose interest unless it is very clear and attractively laid out.

Final Technical Tips

1. There should be *no* errors. Have someone proofread it for spelling, grammar, punctuation, and typographical errors. If an employer finds an error, it usually indicates something to him/her about your performance accuracy.
2. Try to limit yourself to one page. Employers may feel over-

whelmed with too much to read. Say just enough to elicit an interest in interviewing you.

3. Type the original on 8½ x 11 inch paper. Carefully choose your margins and spacing between sections.
4. Use headings to set off each section.
5. Be consistent. Choose a style to describe each section and then maintain it throughout.
6. Be honest! Occasionally employment seekers embellish facts on their résumés. Some employers expect and tolerate exaggeration; however, most employers discount it. Therefore, embellishing the facts will be of little or no value to you.
7. Your final copy should be neat, accurate, concise, errorless, and visually appealing.
8. Type your résumé or have it done professionally on a good quality paper. Do not use a mimeograph machine to make multiple copies. If you choose to have your résumé professionally reproduced, you may have it *typeset* or *offset*. Having a résumé typeset offers variety of composition. The printer can vary the typeface size and shape, thereby creating a visually appealing product. It also allows more information to be printed on the page. It is, however, a more expensive method of reproduction. Offset, on the other hand, is very inexpensive and yields a good, clean reproduction of your original copy. Check around to compare cost and quality before making your decision.
9. Printers may offer you a rainbow of color choices. Traditionally, résumés have been printed on white or off-white paper. Consider where you will be sending the résumé before you choose a color. If in doubt, be conservative.

In summary, your résumé is an effective tool to convey an important message to a prospective employer. *Carefully* plan its content, and *carefully* choose the words and phrases to describe your qualifications.

A well-designed résumé will not only be appreciated by an employer, but it will also aid in the necessary preparation for your interviews.

CHRONOLOGICAL

Rebecca Cerrotti
39 Orlando Avenue
Hometown, U.S.A.
(222) 222-2222

OBJECTIVE: To report and write news stories where creative responsibility is stressed and high motivation is an asset.

NEWS EXPERIENCE:

1983–Present **News Writer**, Internship, WCVB-TV, Needham, MA
Write local, national, and international news for the number one eleven o'clock news program in Boston. Gather news information over the telephone, screen wire copy, distribute scripts, gather slides. Assist sports producer with scores and scripts.

1982 **News Reporter/Stringer**, WTVP, Port David, LA
Covered local news stories and filed reporter packages. Investigated, wrote, and edited soundbites for broadcast.

1980–1982 **News Director/Anchor/Producer**, University Independent Video, Fresno, CA
Supervised a twice weekly, live, half-hour television news program. Responsible for staff of 25 people. Developed news program format. Critiqued writers and reporters, catalogued tapes and visuals, and edited reporter packages for broadcast. As an Anchor and Producer, gathered and formatted news, wrote local, national, and international news.

1981 **Production Assistant Internship**, WABC-TV, New York
Assisted with a daily, live, one-hour news/ public affairs/entertainment program. Researched consumer topics, wrote sports scripts, organized visuals, booked guests, assisted in studio during broadcast.

1980–1981 **News Anchor/Production/Writer**, WERB-AM, Duluth, MN
Anchored and wrote national and international news for daily half-hour newscasts. Formatted news and gathered sound.

1980 **Assistant News Director/Disc Jockey**, WECB-AM, Boston, MA
Organized program schedules, selected staff,

critiqued news scripts. Wrote and anchored news and reports. As Disc Jockey, operated Broadcasting Board, read PSA's, advertisements, and announced records on air.

EDUCATION:
1979–1983

Western College, Provo, UT
Bachelor of Science degree in Mass Communications with a major focus in Broadcast Journalism.

References and tapes available upon request.

FUNCTIONAL

REBECCA CERROTTI
39 Orlando Avenue
Hometown, U.S.A. 02166
(222) 222-2222

QUALIFICATIONS:

Offering a wide range of media skills and knowledge in both the television and radio industry where creative responsibility has been stressed and high motivation has been an asset.

WRITING:

• Able to research, write, critique, and edit news stories on a local, national, and international level for both radio and television markets.
• Created and wrote commercials for a student-run television production.
• As a stringer, wrote and submitted written material for various local newspapers and magazines.
• Assisted sports producer with scripts for sports broadcasts on a local TV network.

PERFORMANCE:

• Anchored a twice weekly, live, half-hour, student-run television news program.
• Anchored news and sports for a student-run AM radio station.
• Performed professionally in 12 piano recitals.

ORGANIZATIONAL/ MANAGEMENT:	• Supervised staff of 25 people to produce a twice weekly, live, half-hour, student-run television news program. • Developed and evaluated news format. • Catalogued tapes, visuals, and slides. • Booked guests for a local TV public affairs/ news/entertainment program. • Organized program schedule. • Selected staff. • Managed finances during four years of college.
EDUCATION:	Bachelor of Science degree in Mass Communications, Arizona State University, Tempe, AZ, May 1983. Major: Broadcast Journalism
INTERESTS:	Classical piano, photography, racquetball.

References and tapes available upon request.

COMBINATION

REBECCA CERROTTI
39 Orlando Avenue
Hometown, U.S.A. 02166
(222) 222-2222

OFFERING:	A highly motivated, self-starting news writer capable of researching, writing, and editing news stories on a local, national, and international level for both television and radio markets.

RADIO EXPERIENCE:

News Reporter	WVIA-FM, Richmond, VA Covered local news stories and filed reporter packages. As a stringer, investigated, wrote and edited soundbites for broadcast. 1982.

News Anchor/Producer/
Writer

WTEX-AM, Waco, TX
Anchored and wrote local, national, and international news for daily half-hour newscasts. Formatted news and gathered sound. 1980–1981.

Assistant News Director/
Disc Jockey

WNM-FM, Westy, NM
Organized program schedules, selected staff, and critiqued news scripts. Wrote and anchored news and sports reports. As a disc jockey, operated broadcasting board, read PSAs and advertisements, and announced records on air. 1979–1980.

**TELEVISION
EXPERIENCE:**

News Writer
Internship

WCVB-TV, Needham, MA
Wrote local, national, and international news for the number one-rated eleven o'clock news program in Boston. Gathered news information over the telephone, screened wire copy, distributed scripts, gathered slides. Assisted sports producer with scores and scripts. 1983–Present.

News Director/
Anchor/Producer

WVOC-AM, Tufte, FL
Supervised twice weekly, live, half-hour television news program. Responsible for a staff of 25 people. Developed news program format. Critiqued writers and reporters, catalogued tapes and visuals, and edited reporter packages for broadcast. As an anchor and producer, gathered and formatted news. Wrote local, national, and international news. 1980–1982.

Production Assistant
Internship

WJIM-FM, Charlotte, NC
Assisted with a daily, live, one-hour, news/public affairs/entertainment program. Researched consumer topics, wrote sports scripts, organized visuals, booked guests, assisted in studio during broadcast. 1981.

EDUCATION:

Bachelor of Science degree in Mass Communications, May 1983.
Arizona State University, Tempe, AZ
Major focus in Broadcast Journalism

Sample Cover Letter

Today's Date

Mr./Ms. Name
Title
Company
and Street Address
City, State, Zip Code

Dear Mr./Ms. Name:

Opening paragraph should arouse enough interest to encourage the reader to press forward. Identify the position you are applying for or inquiring about— how you learned about it (the source). Give information to show your specific interest in this company and this particular position.

Middle paragraph(s) should stimulate desire. Briefly give details of your background—education and experience that will support your candidacy for consideration. Highlight most attractive attributes, and focus on skills required to succeed at the potential job.

How will you use your skills to help the company meet its needs? In what way will you fit into the scheme of things? How can you benefit the employer? Your desire to work for *this* employer must be emphasized. Refer the reader to your enclosed résumé for additional information.

The closing paragraph should indicate your desire to meet to discuss the position. You might state that you are available for an interview at the reader's convenience and that you look forward to hearing from him/her. However, since your goal is to obtain an interview, you should either *ask for one* or *state* that you will *call to arrange one*. A positive request is harder to avoid than a vague hope. And of course, a thank you for one's time and consideration is appropriate.

Sincerely,

Johnny B. Goode
Street Address
City, State, Zip Code

Directory of Communications and Telecommunications Career Information

The purpose of this section is to assist you in defining communications and telecommunications careers. Professional associations, placement services, job listings, and career reference books are the best resources for specific job information.

The following resources will lead you to additional information. Some of the sources merely describe careers; others will give you a broad view of a profession. They are clustered into the following categories:

General
Media
Business
Advertising
Marketing and Sales
Public Relations
Personnel, Human Resources, and Training and Development
Writing and Publishing
Education

GENERAL

CATALYST
14 East 60th Street
New York, NY 10019

Association that focuses upon expanding career options for women by providing career information and self-guidance materials. It facilitates entry into positions and serves as a communications network among women, women's resource centers, employers, educators, and counselors. The Catalyst National Network has more than two hundred local resource centers that offer education, career counseling, and job placement. It also helps employers locate women for directorships. The Career and Family Center deals with problems in two-career families. Catalyst publishes forty self-guidance and career booklets, twelve career options publications for college women, *What to Do with the Rest of Your Life, The Catalyst Career Guide for Women in the 80's*, and guides to résumés and interviews.

COUNCIL OF COMMUNICATION SOCIETIES
P.O. Box 1074
Silver Springs, MD 20910

Organization of professional societies involved in communications. It encourages research and educational programs in communications and provides a center for information about communications organizations. It publishes *Guide to Communication Careers.*

DIRECTORY OF CAREER RESOURCES FOR WOMEN
Alvin Renetzky, Editor in Chief
Ready Reference Press
Santa Monica, CA

Focuses on a wide variety of career opportunities and resources for women. It lists career resources alphabetically and includes a directory of federal job information centers, a subject index, a geographical index, and lists of workshops, talent banks, fellowships, job placement, career development, seminars, reentry programs, nontraditional occupations, apprenticeships, community referral services, career resource libraries, and other information services.

DICTIONARY OF OCCUPATIONAL TITLES
U.S. Department of Labor
Employment and Training Administration
Washington, DC

Lists over 20,000 job descriptions. It is designed as a job placement tool with which individuals may match their skills with the requirements of a particular job.

EXPLORING CAREERS
U.S. Department of Labor
Bureau of Labor Statistics
Washington, DC

Includes articles and resources on all occupations including those in the communications fields.

EXPLORING THEATRE AND MEDIA CAREERS:
A STUDENT HANDBOOK
Michael Allosso and Mary Lewis Hansen
Technical Education Research Centers, Inc.
44 Brattle Street
Cambridge, MA 02138

Covers careers in performance, writing, production, business, education, and criticism. Includes a glossary of communications terms, a list of professional associations, and sources of additional information.

GUIDE FOR OCCUPATIONAL EXPLORATION
U.S. Department of Labor
Employment and Training Administration
Washington, DC

Contains articles and resources on all occupations including those in the communications fields.

HARVARD GUIDE TO CAREERS IN COMMUNICATIONS
Laurie Stauffer
Office of Career Services and Off-Campus Learning
Harvard University
54 Dunster Street
Cambridge, MA 02138

Excellent general source about careers in communications. It includes job descriptions, job environments, techniques of breaking into the field, bibliographies, career information, and professional associations. Its contents focus upon journalism, book publishing, magazine publishing, radio, recording, public relations, advertising, and television/film.

1982 INTERNSHIPS
Edited by Colleen Cannon
Writer's Digest Books
Cincinnati, OH

Excellent resource for internships in many fields including such communications-related fields as advertising, public relations, art, business and industry, education, film, video, government, health, magazines, newspapers, journalism, radio, social service, television, theater, and cultural organizations. It includes regional, national, and international clearinghouses.

JOB BANK BOOKS
Bob Adams, Incorporated
2045 Commonwealth Avenue
Brighton, MA 02135

Comprehensive job reference works that list companies and positions in seven regional books: Texas, Northern California, Pennsylvania, Greater Chicago, Southern California, Metropolitan New York, and Boston.

NATIONAL AD SEARCH
Ad Search, Inc.
2328 West Daphne Road
Milwaukee, WI 53201

Weekly newspaper that publishes over 1,200 advertisements of available jobs that appear in 68 major newspapers, including the New York *Times*, *Wall Street Journal*, and Los Angeles *Times*. Job categories include advertising, communications, design, education, management, marketing, sales, personnel and labor, and agency ads. *Ad Search* is used by individuals, libraries, employment agencies, universities, and federal and state job services.

NATIONAL CAREER DIRECTORY
Barry Gale and Linda Gale
Arco Publishing, Inc.
219 Park Avenue South
New York, NY 10003

A general directory of organizations that provide free or inexpensive materials about careers in many different fields. It lists entrance and training requirements for careers, potential earnings, and the future of the particular field.

NATIONAL JOB-FINDING GUIDE
Heinz Ulrich and J. Robert Connor
Dolphin Books
Doubleday & Company, Inc.
Garden City, NY

Resource that focuses upon job prospects; employment agencies by specialty and location, including communication fields; job opportunities for women, for minorities, for the handicapped; trade and professional journals, the best newspapers for job searching, federal job information centers, state job centers, a listing of 500 major corporations, and how to prepare a résumé.

MEDIA

AMERICAN SOCIETY OF CINEMATOGRAPHERS
1782 North Orange Drive
Hollywood, CA 90028

Organization of professional directors of motion pictures, television photography, and others affiliated with cinematography. Its publications include *American Cinematographer* magazine.

AMERICAN SOCIETY OF TV CAMERAMEN
P.O. Box 296
Sparkill, NY 10976

Association that provides training classes, tours, and seminars to promote standards of professionalism. "Cammy" awards are presented to broadcast and production houses for documentaries and to operations and others in the industry. A placement information service, speakers bureau, and a library are available.

AMERICAN WOMEN IN RADIO AND TELEVISION
1321 Connecticut Avenue, NW
Washington, DC 20036

Organization of professionals involved in work mainly devoted to radio and television. Seminars, career symposia, programs, and forums are held. Children's services, a speakers bureau, and a placement service are provided.

BROADCASTERS' PROMOTION ASSOCIATION
248 West Orange Street
Lancaster, PA 17603

Association of public relations, advertising, and promotion managers of television and radio networks and stations; sponsors an annual On-the-Air competition.

BROADCAST FINANCIAL MANAGEMENT ASSOCIATION
360 North Michigan Avenue
Chicago, IL 60601

Association of persons involved in the financial operations of radio and television to promote and maintain progressive financial management techniques for the broadcasting industry.

BROADCASTING
1735 DeSales Street NW
Washington, DC 20036

Newsweekly that contains extensive lists of jobs in all aspects of broadcasting: announcing, sales, production, programming, management, writing, technical jobs, and others.

BROADCASTING BIBLIOGRAPHY
A Guide to the Literature of Radio and Television
NAB Publications Department
1771 N Street NW
Washington, DC 20036

A major reference bibliography for persons interested in television and radio careers. It covers bibliographies, dictionaries, indexes, books on advertising careers, broadcasting management, programming, engineering, lights, camera, sound, performing, production, reporting, studio, writing, the audience, children, public broadcasting, world broadcasting, cable and pay television, satellites, videotext, periodicals, publishers and distributors.

BROADCASTING YEARBOOK
BROADCASTING
1735 DeSales Street NW
Washington, DC 20036

Lists addresses and information about stations throughout the country.

CABLEVISION
Titsch Publishing Incorporated
2500 Curtis Street
Denver, CO 80217

Magazine devoted to news about the cable television industry. An Employment Opportunities/Help Wanted section includes job descriptions and employment agencies that handle placement in cable television.

CAREERLINE
American Women in Radio and Television
1321 Connecticut Avenue NW
Washington, DC 20036

Toll-free service that lists job openings in radio and television across the nation.

CAREERS IN BROADCASTING NEWS, 3d ed.
Vernon Stone
Radio-Television News Directors Association
1735 DeSales Street NW
Washington, DC 20036

Pamphlet that describes the profession of news broadcasting. Topics include the nature of change in broadcast news, the future, what broadcast journalists do, a listing of job types, pay, educational preparation, and getting one's first job.

DIRECTORS GUILD OF AMERICA
7950 Sunset Boulevard
Hollywood, CA 90046

Union of directors of motion pictures and television productions. It publishes *Action* and *Director of Members*.

EMPLOYMENT CLEARINGHOUSE
National Association of Broadcasters
1771 N Street NW
Washington, DC 20036

Advisory service helping women and minorities to enter the broadcast industry through career counseling and job referrals.

EXPLORING CAREERS IN BROADCAST JOURNALISM
Rod Vahl
The Rosen Publishing Group, New York, NY 10010

A career book on opportunities in broadcast journalism.

EXPLORING CAREERS IN CABLE/TV
David Berlyn
The Rosen Publishing Group, New York, NY 10010

Covers programming, news, management, engineering, sales, promotion, and the latest on cable

EXPLORING CAREERS IN FILMMAKING
Robert Manning
The Rosen Publishing Group, New York, NY 10010

All the information you need to lead you to a career in filmmaking.

EXPLORING CAREERS IN VIDEO
Paul Allman
The Rosen Publishing Group, New York, NY 10010

Career opportunities for those with the right qualifications.

EXPLORING CAREERS: JOBS IN COMMUNICATIONS
Edward Wakin
Lothrop, Lee & Shepard Company
New York, NY

Career book dealing with the broad aspects of mass communications.

*FOCAL ENCYCLOPEDIA OF FILM AND
TELEVISION TECHNIQUES*
Hastings House Publishers
New York, NY 10016

A comprehensive source of definitions and techniques for film and television including such topics as lighting, film storage, processing, screen luminance, sound recording, special effects, telecine (color), cutting, documentary filming, and many other principles.

GUIDE TO PROFESSIONAL RADIO AND TV NEWSCASTING
Robert C. Siller
TAB Books
Blue Ridge Summit, PA 17214

Discusses equipment, voice, appearance, preparation, writing, marketing, and timing of television news, reporting, and the interview.

THE HOLLYWOOD TV PRODUCER:
HIS WORK AND AUDIENCE
Muriel G. Cantor
Basic Books, Inc.
New York, NY

Describes the role of television producer and what he or she must know.

INTERMEDIA
475 Riverside Drive
New York, NY 10115

Organization that coordinates missionary agencies involved in improving literacy around the world through audiovisual production centers, radio and television programming and operations, publishing houses and bookstores, and workshops.

INTERNATIONAL RADIO AND TELEVISION SOCIETY
420 Lexington Avenue
New York, NY 10170

Society of professionals involved in the management and sales production of radio and television broadcasting and related fields. Offers internships for college students.

MEDIA RESEARCH DIRECTORS ASSOCIATION
Earl G. Graves, Ltd.
295 Madison Avenue
New York, NY 10017

Organization of research directors of national print and broadcast media. Scholarship awards are presented to media/marketing researchers and business school undergraduates. Placement service is available.

NATIONAL ACADEMY OF TELEVISION ARTS AND SCIENCES
110 West 57th Street
New York, NY 10019

Organization of professionals engaged in all phases of television production. The advancement of the television industry is recognized by the Emmy awards. College students may become student affiliate members and may attend special events twice a month to meet television professionals.

NATIONAL ASSOCIATION OF BROADCASTERS
1771 N Street NW
Washington, DC 20036

Major organization that represents radio and television stations, national networks, and producers of programs and equipment. It sets up guidelines (voluntary) for acceptable programming and advertising practices. It publishes *Careers in Radio*, *Careers in Television*, and *Broadcasting Bibliography*.

NATIONAL ASSOCIATION OF FARM BROADCASTERS
P.O. Box 119
Topeka, KS 66601

Association for radio and television farm directors who promote the broadcasting of farm news and information, and all other persons involved with farming advertising and government and commercial organizations. Placement information is provided.

NATIONAL CABLE TELEVISION ASSOCIATION
1724 Massachusetts Avenue NW
Washington, DC 20036

Membership includes cable systems and related distributors, firms, institutions, and manufacturers. Cooperation is maintained with many other cable television associations. Standards of conduct for personnel and management are developed as well as publications, study, and research.

NATIONAL RADIO BROADCASTERS ASSOCIATION
1705 DeSales Street NW
Washington, DC 20036

Organization of radio stations and firms in related broadcasting industries to promote time sales, increase radio audiences, and participate in government legislation.

PACT (People and Careers in Telecommunications)
National Association of Educational Broadcasters
1346 Connecticut Avenue NW
Washington, DC 20036

Publishes *PACTsheet*, a free, biweekly job bulletin announcing positions available in public television and radio section management, technical fields, and education and instructional media.

ORGANIZATIONS, PUBLICATIONS, AND DIRECTORIES
IN THE MASS MEDIA OF COMMUNICATIONS
School of Journalism
University of Iowa
Iowa City, Iowa

Lists organizations and their publications, business and professional publications, directories, names and addresses of state press and broadcasting agencies-associations, and other facts about media.

RADIO ADVERTISING BUREAU
485 Lexington Avenue
New York, NY 10017

Organization of radio networks, stations, and sales representatives. Offers a program to improve the professionalism of radio salespeople. The designation of Certified Radio Marketing Consultant is awarded to those who pass an examination. Conducts regional conferences on programming, promotion, sales, and general management, and a research program on commercial awareness and trends in media.

RADIO TELEVISION NEWS DIRECTORS ASSOCIATION
1735 DeSales Street NW
Washington, DC 20036

Professional organization for persons involved in the gathering, editing, and presenting of news. It sponsors an international conference and a series of spring regional conferences, operates a placement service and a speakers bureau and publishes a career booklet.

ROSS REPORTS TELEVISION
Television Index
150 Fifth Avenue
New York, NY 10011

Source of detailed information on script and casting requirements of continuing television programs, including how and when to submit work.

SCREEN ACTORS GUILD (SAG)
7750 Sunset Boulevard
Hollywood, CA 90046

Union of actors in the motion picture industry; member of the AFL-CIO. It publishes the quarterly magazine *Screen Actor*.

SOCIETY OF BROADCAST ENGINEERS
7002 Graham Road
Indianapolis, IN 46220

The broadcast professionals, engineers, and students of this organization provide an information exchange, hold a certification program, encourage the professional abilities of members, and are represented at the Federal Communications Commission.

SOCIETY OF MOTION PICTURE AND
TELEVISION ENGINEERS (SMPTE)
862 Scarsdale Avenue
Scarsdale, NY 10583

Professional organization dedicated to advancing the engineering and technical aspects of the motion picture, television, and allied arts and sciences. College students may become members if recommended by an SMPTE member or a faculty member. Student members may attend monthly local chapter meetings and national conferences and receive the SMPTE *Journal* and *News & Notes*.

TELEVISION INFORMATION OFFICE
745 Fifth Avenue
New York, NY 10022

Office formed to open communication between the general public and the television industry. The National Association of Broadcasters and television networks and stations dispense information for education in these areas. Research studies are commissioned, and a library of books and files on television is maintained.

TV AND RADIO CAREERS
D. X. Fenten
Franklin Watts, Inc.
New York, NY

Covers programming, producing, directing, broadcast engineering, sales, and an extensive list of professional schools, colleges, and universities offering programs and courses in radio and television.

VIDEO TRAINING PROGRAM
Institute for New Cinema Artists
62 West 45th Street
New York, NY 10036

Program for qualified minorities. A placement service is offered to graduates.

WOMEN IN CABLE
2053 M Street NW
Washington, DC 20036

Organization of professionals involved in cable television and related areas, dedicated to exchanges of ideas, opinions, and standards of professionalism. Career development, internship, and educational programs are conducted.

WOMEN'S AND MINORITY TRAINING GRANTS
Corporation for Public Broadcasting
1111 16th Street NW
Washington, DC 20036

These grants are awarded to CPB-licensed television and radio stations and associated production centers. Stations must pay at least one-half of a trainee's salary, benefits and training costs for one to two years.

BUSINESS

AMERICAN MANAGEMENT ASSOCIATIONS
135 West 50th Street
New York, NY 10020

Organization of nearly 100,000 managers in business, government, and nonprofit organizations as well as university teachers and administrators. It has an extensive library and a Management Information Service that maintains films, cassettes, tapes, and records covering planning, development, training, general management, human resources, information technology, marketing, packaging, research, and insurance. It also sponsors the Society for the Advancement of Management, with chapters in schools and colleges.

ASSOCIATION FOR SYSTEMS MANAGEMENT
24587 Bagley Road
Cleveland, OH 44138

Organization of executives and persons who specialize in management information systems. It is concerned with communications, electronics, human relations, organization, procedure writing, and systems applications and offers seminars and conferences on administrative systems and management.

BUSINESS INFORMATION SOURCES
Lorna M. Daniels
University of California Press
Berkeley, Los Angeles, London

Directory of information sources on business careers. Includes bibliographies, directories, business dictionaries, indexes, government publications, computerized information services, handbooks, company directories, and directories of trade names, associations, periodicals, and research centers.

CAREER EMPLOYMENT OPPORTUNITIES DIRECTORY
Volume 2, Business Administration
Alvin Renetzky, Editor in Chief
Ready Reference Press
Santa Monica, CA

Guide to careers in business including those related to communications such as administration, industrial relations, management, marketing, personnel, and public relations.

INDUSTRIAL COMMUNICATION COUNCIL
P.O. Box 3970, Grand Central Station
New York, NY 10163

Organization of persons who work in business and organizational communications. Provides workshops and seminars, a speakers bureau, and placement services.

INTERNATIONAL ASSOCIATION OF
BUSINESS COMMUNICATORS
870 Market Street
San Francisco, CA 94102

Association of nearly 10,000 persons involved in all phases of business communication: management, advertising, writers, editors, audiovisual specialists, organizational communications. It offers over fifty annual seminars, publishes *Journal of Organizational Communication* and *Directory of Business and Organizational Communicators*, and provides a telephone placement service, Jobline.

INTERNATIONAL COMMUNICATIONS ASSOCIATION
9550 Forest Lane
Dallas, TX 75243

Association of persons responsible for telecommunication services in major organizations such as those that need to communicate with multicity offices.

NATIONAL ASSOCIATION OF BUSINESS
AND EDUCATIONAL RADIO
1330 New Hampshire Avenue
Washington, DC 20036

Association of organizations that are licensed to use two-way radio under the business radio service regulations of the FCC. It publishes statistics on business radio users.

NATIONAL BUSINESS EMPLOYMENT WEEKLY
Published by the *Wall Street Journal*
Box 300
Princeton, NJ 08540

A resource of job information in business communication, corporate communication, advertising, personnel, human resources, training, management, marketing, and labor relations. It carries articles on such topics as prospects for jobs in particular fields, career events calendar, negotiating salary, and novel job-hunting tactics.

SOCIETY FOR ADVANCEMENT OF MANAGEMENT
135 West 50th Street
New York, NY 10020

Division of the American Management Associations. It sponsors many college and university chapters and is a good career starting point for all management careers including collective bargaining, quality control, training, marketing, industrial relations, and entrepreneurship.

ADVERTISING

ADVERTISING CAREERS
Harry C. Groome Jr.
National Textbook Company
8259 Niles Center Road
Skokie, IL 60077

Concentrates on advertising agencies, their structure, job descriptions of the people who work in agencies, and opportunities.

ADVERTISING COUNCIL
825 Third Avenue
New York, NY 10022

Organization formed by businesses, media, and advertisers to support national causes. Some of the campaigns it has supported include energy conservation, crime and forest fire prevention, Peace Corps, United Way, World Hunger, Aid to Higher Education, United Negro College Fund, and Action.

ADVERTISING PRODUCTION CLUB OF NEW YORK
15 Vanderbilt Avenue
New York, NY 10017

Organization of advertising personnel involved in production and traffic departments. It sponsors educational programs in graphics in advertising and provides a placement service. It also grants scholarships in graphics to the New York City Technical College and Printing Industries of Metropolitan New York.

ADVERTISING RESEARCH FOUNDATION
3 East 54th Street
New York, NY 10022

Organization of advertising agencies, advertisers, associations, research organizations, and the media, with colleges and universities as associate members. Maintains an information center and publishes *Journal of Advertising Research.*

ADVERTISING WOMEN OF NEW YORK
153 East 57th Street
New York, NY 10022

Organization of women on an executive and administrative level in all phases of advertising and marketing. Personal job counseling is provided, and career conferences, scholarships, and other educational programs are funded.

AMERICAN ADVERTISING FEDERATION
1225 Connecticut Avenue NW
Washington, DC 20036

Organization of trade associations, advertising clubs, students, advertisers, and the media. Its primary objective is to further the understanding of advertising through self-regulation and public relations. The Federation publishes *Job Clearinghouse.*

AMERICAN ASSOCIATION OF ADVERTISING AGENCIES
666 Third Avenue
New York, NY 10017

Known as the "4 A's," the association works to improve advertising content, cooperates with government agencies in legislative and regulatory matters, and maintains standards of service for agencies. It supports academic research in advertising and helps college educators do a better job of teaching advertising and marketing. It publishes *Advertising: A Guide to Careers in Advertising*, and *Advertising Agencies: What They Are, What They Do, And How They Do It.*

AMERICAN INSTITUTE OF GRAPHIC ARTS
1059 Third Avenue
New York, NY 10021

Association of graphic designers, package designers, illustrators, and art directors involved in printing and other graphic fields. It conducts book clinics and seminars.

ASSOCIATION OF NATIONAL ADVERTISERS
155 East 44th Street
New York, NY 10017

Association that holds workshops, seminars, surveys, and studies. A placement service and specialized education are provided.

BUSINESS/PROFESSIONAL ADVERTISING ASSOCIATION
205 East 42nd Street
New York, NY 10017

Members include students and educators along with business communications professionals in advertising, marketing, and marketing communications. Seminars are held, and an employment service is operated by headquarters and by local chapters. Publications include *Communicator*, the annual *Directory*, periodic special reports, and *Communications Report*.

ENCYCLOPEDIA OF ADVERTISING
by Irvin Graham
Fairchild Publications, Inc.
New York, N.Y.

A comprehensive reference source that contains over 1,000 terms related to advertising, marketing, publishing, public relations, publicity, and graphic arts.

EXPLORING CAREERS IN ADVERTISING
Larry Deckinger
Jules B. Singer
The Rosen Publishing Group
29 East 21st Street
New York, NY 10010

Career book that discusses the nature of advertising, education needed, the workings of an agency, and opportunities in advertising including magazines, newspapers, radio, television, and trade papers.

SPECIALTY ADVERTISING ASSOCIATION INTERNATIONAL
1404 Walnut Hill Lane
Irving, TX 75062

Organization of direct selling houses of imprinted specialties and executive gifts. Provides an information and speakers bureau of specialty advertising, development seminars, and sales institutes.

STANDARD DIRECTORY OF ADVERTISING AGENCIES
National Register Publishing Company
5201 Old Orchard Road
Skokie, IL 60076

Lists over 4,000 agencies and the accounts they handle.

TELEVISION BUREAU OF ADVERTISING
485 Lexington Avenue
New York, NY 10017

Organization of television networks, program producers and syndicators, and sales representatives involved in the promotion of television as an advertising medium. Sales materials and film presentations are produced, audience composition studies are held, and research on the processes of communications is conducted.

WHERE SHALL I GO TO COLLEGE
TO STUDY ADVERTISING?
Advertising Education Publications
3429 Fifty-fifth Street
Lubbock, TX 79413

Listing of schools with advertising programs.

MARKETING AND SALES

BANK MARKETING ASSOCIATION
309 West Washington Street
Chicago, IL 60606

Organization that provides printed materials and visual aids on banking and marketing and conducting workshops, seminars, courses, and summer sessions. It maintains an information center and houses materials on public relations, marketing, and advertising. It also offers a placement service and publishes the *Bank Marketing Journal.*

DIRECT MAIL/MARKETING ASSOCIATION
6 East 43rd Street
New York, NY 10017

Organization of groups and individuals associated with direct mail advertising and marketing, including envelope manufacturers, lettershops, computer mailing list services, printers, and designers of direct mail advertisements. It provides seminars and sponsors direct mail competition and awards.

DIRECT SELLING EDUCATIONAL FOUNDATION
1730 M Street NW
Washington, DC 20036

Organization that focuses upon improving consumer communications through computers and satellite technology. It cosponsors consumer education conferences with universities.

HAVE YOU CONSIDERED SALES
Catalyst
14 East 60th Street
New York, NY 10022

Publication that deals with personality characteristics, opportunities, options available to the sales worker, educational preparation, lifestyle options, and the current employment market.

MARKETING COMMUNICATIONS
EXECUTIVES INTERNATIONAL
1831 Chestnut Street
Philadelphia, PA 19103

Association of executives involved with the supervision, planning, and direct execution of marketing communications and of teachers of marketing communications. It provides a speakers bureau and an employment service.

MARKETING RESEARCH ASSOCIATION
221 North LaSalle Street
Chicago, IL 60601

Organization of persons involved in marketing research for advertising agencies. It distributes research guidelines, manuals, and an Interviewer Training Film.

NATIONAL AGRI-MARKETING ASSOCIATION
8340 Mission Road
Prairie Village, KS 66206

Organization of persons who work in marketing and agricultural advertising. It promotes high standards of agricultural marketing and encourages the study of agricultural advertising through sponsorship of competitions.

NATIONAL ASSOCIATION OF MARKET DEVELOPERS
201 Ashby Street NW
Atlanta, GA 30314

Organization that focuses on marketing to minorities, including sales, publishing, advertising, and public relations. It provides a placement service and a speakers bureau.

SALES AND MARKETING EXECUTIVES INTERNATIONAL
380 Lexington Avenue
New York, NY 10168

Organization of executives involved in sales and marketing. It sponsors a Sales Management Institute, workshops and seminars, and career programs and works with the Junior Achievement and Distributive Education Clubs of America to interest youth in sales and marketing careers.

SALES EXECUTIVES CLUB OF NEW YORK
122 East 42nd Street
New York, NY 10168

Organization of executives who wish to seek better ways to market and sell products. It provides seminars and works with schools and colleges. The Sales Manpower Foundation compiles information about available sales executives and personnel and publishes *Job Opening Lists* and "How to Land the Job You Want."

YOUR FUTURE IN MARKETING
Norman B. Orent
Richards Rosen Press
29 East 21st Street
New York, NY 10010

The education, training and techniques to make a marketing success.

PUBLIC RELATIONS

AMERICAN BUSINESS PRESS
205 East 42nd Street
New York, NY 10017

Organization of publishers of institutional and business magazines and newspapers. It provides information on advertising agencies and promotional aids and an employment service.

AMERICAN PUBLICISTS GUILD
13415 Ventura Boulevard
Sherman Oaks, CA 91423

Organization of writers of publicity as a field distinct from advertising and public relations.

AMERICAN SOCIETY OF BUSINESS EDITORS
435 North Michigan Avenue
Chicago, IL 60611

Organization of editors of business, trade, and technical publications. It provides educational programs in conjunction with educational institutions and journalism associations and a limited placement service.

CAREERS IN PUBLIC RELATIONS
Public Relations Society of America
845 Third Avenue
New York, NY 10022

Describes the nature of public relations in today's society, salary levels, the kind of work performed by a PR person, the personal and academic qualifications needed, and the various fields of public relations, including businesses, associations, labor unions, schools and colleges, volunteer agencies, government, and public relations firms.

EXPLORING CAREERS IN PUBLIC RELATIONS
Edward Bernays
The Rosen Publishing Group
29 East 21st Street
New York, NY 10010

The founder of public relations tells the true value and worth of a public relations career and how to achieve it.

FOUNDATION FOR PUBLIC RELATIONS RESEARCH AND EDUCATION
415 Lexington Avenue
New York, NY 10017

The foundation sponsors and conducts research in public relations; it offers fellowships to university teachers of public relations and undergraduate and graduate scholarships to students. It publishes *Public Relations: A Comprehensive Bibliography*, *Public Relations Review*, and *Managing Your Public Relations*.

HANDBOOK ON INTERNATIONAL PUBLIC RELATIONS
Prepared by Executives and Associates of
Hill and Knowlton International
Frederic A. Praeger, Publishers
New York, Washington, London

Describes international public relations in the countries of Western Europe, covering such topics as the history of public relations, communications media, financial public relations, government public relations, and the relation between companies and their various publics.

INSTITUTE OF PERSONAL IMAGE CONSULTANTS
Editorial Services Company
1140 Avenue of the Americas
New York, NY 10036

Organization of persons who do training and consulting in the area of personal image improvement such as speed training, personal public relations, dress coordination and selection. It publishes *Directory of Personal Image Consultants*.

INTERNATIONAL PUBLIC RELATIONS ASSOCIATION
c/o Illinois Bell
225 West Randolph Street
Chicago, IL 60606

Organization of persons from over fifty countries in the field of public relations. It has its international headquarters in London.

LESLY'S PUBLIC RELATIONS HANDBOOK, 2d ed.
Edited by Philip Lesly
Prentice-Hall Inc.
Englewood Cliffs, N.J.

Comprehensive handbook on public relations, it includes sections on the role of public relations, effective communication, working with government, communities, and minorities, financial public relations, industry relations, employee relations and communications, labor, marketing, dealer relations, consumer relations, television, radio, motion pictures, direct communication methods, influential groups, religious groups, retailers, nonprofit organizations, newspapers, and international public relations.

NATIONAL SCHOOL PUBLIC RELATIONS ASSOCIATION
1801 North Moore Street
Arlington, VA 22209

Organization of school system public relations directors and school administrators. It publishes books, reports, public relations aids, and handbooks.

NEW YORK/INTERNATIONAL ASSOCIATION OF
BUSINESS COMMUNICATORS
P.O. Box 2025, Grand Central Station
New York, NY 10017

Organization of organizational communicators in the New York area, including printers, managers of communications departments, publishers, company editors, and producers of audiovisual materials. It offers a communicator service for beginners, sponsors workshops, and provides a placement bureau.

O'DWYER'S DIRECTORY OF
CORPORATE COMMUNICATIONS
J. R. O'Dwyer Co., Inc.
271 Madison Avenue
New York, NY 10016

A major reference work in the field of corporate communications, the directory lists about 2,500 companies with corporate communications departments. The contents include corporations grouped by type of industry, geographical index to headquarters of corporations, and corporations and associations listed in alphabetical order.

O'DWYER'S DIRECTORY OF PUBLIC RELATIONS FIRMS
J. R. O'Dwyer Co., Inc.
271 Madison Avenue
New York, NY 10016

A major reference resource for persons interested in public relations careers as well as associated careers such as writing, media, management, and all forms of communications. It lists and ranks the major public relations firms, both independently owned firms and those owned by advertising agencies. It includes an index to public relations firms with specialized skills, a geographical index of public relations firms, an index to advertisers by type of service, an alphabetical index to advertisers, a section on how to hire an outside PR counsel, and an alphabetical list of public relations firms.

PUBLIC RELATIONS: INFORMATION SOURCES
Alice Norton
Gale Research Company
Book Tower
Detroit, Michigan

A comprehensive resource for books in the field of public relations. It includes handbooks and dictionaries, directories, encyclopedic articles, free materials, speeches, periodicals, public relations libraries, and basic books selected by the Public Relations Society of America. It also includes public relations tools such as attitude and marketing research, publicity, public relations services, special events, practical advice for the writer, printing, exhibitions, mass media, the press, public relations associations, careers in public relations, and information about international public relations.

PUBLIC RELATIONS SOCIETY OF AMERICA
845 Third Avenue
New York, NY 10022

Organization of persons from business, public relations counseling firms, government agencies, educational institutions, trade andprofessional groups, and nonprofit organizations. The PRSA has an Accreditation Program and conducts programs in continuing education. It publishes *Public Relations Journal, Public Relations Yearbook*, an annual public relations bibliography, a list of colleges offering degrees and courses in public relations, and *Careers in Public Relations*. It also maintains an executive referral service.

PUBLIC RELATIONS STUDENT SOCIETY OF AMERICA
Public Relations Society of America
845 Third Avenue
New York, NY 10022

Organization affiliated with the PRSA. It brings together students of public relations and professionals.

PERSONNEL, HUMAN RESOURCES, AND TRAINING AND DEVELOPMENT

ADMINISTRATIVE MANAGEMENT SOCIETY
Maryland Road
Willow Grove, PA 19090

Association of persons involved in information management, personnel systems, and administrative services. It focuses on methods of improving productivity while lowering costs and assists institutions in developing training programs.

AMERICAN PERSONNEL AND GUIDANCE ASSOCIATION
2 Skyline Place
5203 Leesburg Pike
Falls Church, VA 22041

With approximately 40,000 members, this is the largest association of personnel and guidance workers in all profit and nonprofit organizations. It maintains a placement service and publishes *Placement Service Review*, *Journal of Employment Counseling*, and *Vocational Guidance* quarterly. It has such divisions as college personnel, rehabilitation counseling, measurement and evaluation, minority concerns, employment counseling, and vocational guidance.

AMERICAN SOCIETY FOR PERSONNEL ADMINISTRATION
30 Park Drive
Berea, OH 44017

Organization of personnel and industrial executives. It provides a personnel placement service and seminars for personnel administrators and publishes books and other materials on human resources.

AMERICAN SOCIETY FOR TRAINING AND DEVELOPMENT
600 Maryland Avenue SW
Washington, DC 20025

Educational association of persons involved in the training and development of personnel in business, education, and government. It provides institutes for training professionals, a member inquiry service, an Operation Talent Match, a Position Referral Service, and a division of Career Development.

.

HUMAN RESOURCE PLANNING SOCIETY
P.O. Box 2553, Grand Central Station
New York, NY 10163

Organization of human resource professionals, planning and development specialists, staffing analysts, and other individuals involved with personnel and human resources management.

INDUSTRIAL RELATIONS AND PERSONNEL MANAGEMENT:

Selected Information Sources
Martha Jane Soltow and Jo Ann Stehberger Sokkar
Scarecrow Press, Inc.
Metuchen, N.J., London

Contains a listing of resources in the field of personnel, bibliographies, biographical information, dictionaries, indexes, special collections, research organizations, professional organizations, arbitration, collective bargaining, and occupational safety and health.

INDUSTRIAL RELATIONS RESEARCH ASSOCIATION
7225 Social Science Building
University of Wisconsin
Madison, WI 53706

Organization of over 5,000 business union leaders, lawyers, arbitrators, and teachers interested in research on labor relations and personnel administration.

INTERNATIONAL PERSONNEL MANAGEMENT ASSOCIATION
1850 K Street NW
Washington, DC 20006

Organization of persons in government and public-sector personnel work. It provides testing services, advisory services, conferences, and development programs; offers a limited placement service, and publishes the Public Employee Relations Library.

NATIONAL MANAGEMENT ASSOCIATION
2210 Arbor Boulevard
Dayton, OH 45439

Organization of business and industrial supervisors and middle managers. It provides programs on management, communications, human behavior, industrial relations, and liberal education.

PERSONNEL MANAGEMENT
by William J. Traynor
National Textbook Company
8259 Niles Center Road
Skokie, IL 60077

Describes the fast-growing field of personnel work, including qualifications for the job and opportunities for advancement.

WRITING AND PUBLISHING

AMERICAN BUSINESS PRESS
205 East 42nd Street
New York, NY 10017

Organization of publishers of institutional and business magazines and newspapers. It provides information on advertising agencies and promotional aids, and an employment service.

AMERICAN MEDICAL WRITERS' ASSOCIATION
5272 River Road
Bethesda, MD 20816

Organization of medical writers, editors, publishers, audiovisual specialists, and other persons involved in medical communications. It publishes *Journal of Medical Communications*, *Membership Directory*, and *Freelance Directory*.

AMERICAN NEWSPAPER PUBLISHERS ASSOCIATION
11600 Sunrise Valley Drive
Reston, VA 22091

Service organization that provides information on circulation, management, employee relations, labor matters, news research, and telecommunications. In Easton, Pennsylvania, it has a library of 5,000 volumes on mass communications, newspapers, and journalism.

AMERICAN NEWS WOMEN'S CLUB
1607 22nd Street NW
Washington, DC 20008

Organization of women newswriters in all media, government, and profit and nonprofit organizations.

AMERICAN PLACE THEATRE
111 West 46th Street
New York, NY 10036

Organization that seeks to provide opportunities for authors to develop new plays. It stages productions, provides professional consultation, and hosts post-play discussions.

AMERICAN PLAYWRIGHTS THEATRE
1102 Drake Union
Ohio State University
1849 Cannon Drive
Columbus, OH 43210

Organization that provides playwrights with opportunities to try out new plays and new forms of theater in educational and community settings. It is supported by the American Educational Theatre Association and the American National Theatre and Academy.

AMERICAN PUBLICISTS GUILD
13415 Ventura Boulevard
Sherman Oaks, CA 91423

Organization of writers of publicity as distinct from advertising and public relations writers.

AMERICAN SOCIETY OF BUSINESS EDITORS
435 North Michigan Avenue
Chicago, IL 60611

Organization of editors of business, trade, and technical publications. It provides educational programs in conjunction with educational institutions and journalism associations and a limited placement service.

AMERICAN SOCIETY OF JOURNALISTS AND AUTHORS
1501 Broadway
New York, NY 10036

Organization of free-lance nonfiction writers. It provides a Dial-A-Writer Service for writers.

AMERICAN WRITERS THEATRE FOUNDATION
P.O. Box 810, Times Square Station
New York, NY 10108

Organization that encourages new works and adaptations of masterpieces for the stage. Workshops and productions are produced by its membership of theater professionals from community, university, and regional theaters.

ASSOCIATED WRITING PROGRAMS
Old Dominion University
Norfolk, VA 23508

Organization of students, teachers, writers, and small press editors. It assists writers in finding employment and in getting published. It provides a placement service and publishes a *Catalogue of Programs* that describes writing programs in over 250 institutions.

BOOK PUBLISHERS DIRECTORY
Edited by Annie M. Brewer and Elizabeth A. Geiser
Gale Research Company
Book Tower
Detroit, MI 48226

Guide to new and established, private and special-interest, avant-garde and alternative, government and institutional presses.

CAREERS IN BOOK PUBLISHING
McGraw-Hill, Inc.
1221 Avenue of the Americas
New York, NY 10020

Booklet describing the careers of persons who plan, edit, design, produce, and market books. It includes job descriptions, types of publishing, and the preparation required to enter the field.

EXPLORING CAREERS IN JOURNALISM
Thomas Pawlick
The Rosen Publishing Group
29 East 21st Street
New York, NY 10010

FEMINIST WRITERS GUILD
P.O. Box 9396
Berkeley, CA 94709

Organization of women to share information and experiences about writing and ways of getting published. It publishes *Feminist Writers' Guild Handbook on How to Get Published and Get Paid.*

FICTION WRITER'S MARKET
Edited by John Brady and Jean M. Fredette
Writer's Digest Books
9933 Alliance Road
Cincinnati, OH 45242

Focuses primarily on the fiction writer's market, with articles about writers' habits, the business of fiction writing, agents, literary magazines, small presses, commercial publishers, writers' organizations, and an index to markets.

FREE-LANCE WRITING
Hazel Carter Maxon
National Textbook Company
8259 Niles Center Road
Skokie, IL 60077

Discusses how to select marketable nonfiction material, prepare manuscripts, circulate articles among publishers, and evaluate offers.

INTERNATIONAL WOMEN'S WRITING GUILD
Box 810, Gracie Station
New York, NY 10028

Organization devoted to giving guidance and encouragement to established and aspiring women writers. It sponsors writers' conferences, helps with the submission of manuscripts, and has a job placement "talent bank."

JOURNALISM CAREER AND SCHOLARSHIP GUIDE
Dow Jones Newspaper Fund, Inc.
P.O. Box 3000
Princeton, NJ 08540

Comprehensive resource for persons interested in journalism careers. It includes a communications media employment report, newspaper salary report, college courses, jobs beyond writing and editing, applying for a newspaper job, tips from editors, directory of scholarships and journalism colleges, listing of colleges that offer majors in journalism/mass communication and scholarships, minority grants and other scholarships, internships, and awards, and an index of schools.

LITERARY MARKETPLACE: THE DIRECTORY OF AMERICAN BOOK PUBLISHING
R.R. Bowker Company
1180 Avenue of the Americas
New York, NY 10036

Directory of book clubs, associations, book trade events, courses, conferences, contests, agents, agencies, direct mail, radio.

MAGAZINE INDUSTRY MARKETPLACE
R.R. Bowker Company
1180 Avenue of the Americas
New York, NY 10036

Focuses on the writers' market in magazine publishing. It classifies each area by type of publication and by subject matter such as advertising, automotive, computers, communication arts, and culture.

MAGAZINE PUBLISHERS ASSOCIATION
575 Lexington Avenue
New York, NY 10022

Organization of publishers of consumer magazines. It provides a Publishers Information Bureau and maintains a comprehensive library on magazine work.

NATIONAL ASSOCIATION OF SCIENCE WRITERS
P.O. Box 294
Greenlawn, NY 11740

Association of writers and editors of scientific news. It has a vocational committee and a Free Lance Committee. It also publishes *Guide to Careers in Science Writing* and *Handbook for Press Arrangements at Scientific Meetings.*

NATIONAL FEDERATION OF PRESS WOMEN
Box 99
Blue Springs, MS 64015

Federation of state organizations of women *and men* in communications and journalism. It conducts contests, provides educational programs, and offers scholarships in journalism.

NATIONAL PLAYWRIGHTS CONFERENCE
1860 Broadway
New York, NY 10023

Program sponsored by the Eugene O'Neill Memorial Theatre Center for writers. Over 1,000 scripts are reviewed, and twelve to fourteen plays and four scripts are chosen for work at the conference.

NATIONAL PRESS CLUB
529 14th Street NW
Washington, DC 20045

Organization of news reporters and writers working for newspapers, magazines, television, radio, and networks.

NATIONAL WRITERS CLUB
1450 South Havana
Aurora, CO 80012

Association of persons who have published books, plays, scripts, and magazine articles. It publishes *Freelancers' Market, Flash Market News, Authorship,* and special reports.

NEWSWOMEN'S CLUB OF NEW YORK
600 Lexington Avenue
New York, NY 10022

Association of women journalists working in newspapers, wire services, newsmagazines, and television or radio networks that originate in New York. It grants scholarships to the Columbia School of Journalism and travel-work scholarships.

NEW YORK/INTERNATIONAL ASSOCIATION OF
BUSINESS COMMUNICATORS
P.O. Box 2025, Grand Central Station
New York, NY 10017

Organization of organizational communicators in the New York area
including printers, managers of communication departments, publishers, company editors, and producers of audiovisual materials. It offers
a communicator service to beginners, sponsors workshops, and provides a placement bureau.

OPPORTUNITIES IN GRAPHIC COMMUNICATIONS—
THE PRINTING INDUSTRY
George Reinfeld, Jr.
National Textbook Company
8259 Niles Center Road
Skokie, IL 60077

Introduction to the printing industry, how to get started, and a classifi-
cation of jobs in the industry. It has a list of schools that offer courses
and degrees in graphic communication.

OPPORTUNITIES IN TECHNICAL WRITING TODAY
Jay R. Gould and Wayne A. Losano
National Textbook Company
8259 Niles Road
Skokie, IL 60077

Focuses on the types of jobs available in scientific and technical writing
and the education necessary to obtain such positions.

OPPORTUNITIES IN WRITING CAREERS
Elizabeth Foote-Smith
National Textbook Company
8259 Niles Center Road
Skokie, IL 60077

Deals with markets for original writing and writing on "spec" and
addresses issues such as dealing with publishers and agents.

OVERSEAS PRESS CLUB OF AMERICA
52 East 41st Street
New York, NY 10017

Organization of journalists now serving or having served overseas, including correspondents, editors, reporters, photographers, and freelance writers. It provides public information, exhibits, forums, archives, and research. It also maintains a placement service and provides youth and student activities.

ROMANCE WRITERS OF AMERICA
P.O. Box 90012
Houston, TX 77090

Association of authors, editors, and publishers of romance novels. It conducts workshops and manuscript analysis for beginning and advanced authors.

SCIENCE FICTION WRITERS OF AMERICA
c/o Peter D. Pautz
68 Countryside Apartments
Hackettstown, NJ 07840

Organization of science fiction writers. It promotes public interest in science fiction and conducts conferences, lectures, and seminars. It publishes *Directory of the Science Fiction Writers of America.*

WOMEN'S NATIONAL BOOK ASSOCIATION
The Public Library of
Nashville and Davidson Company
Eighth and Union
Nashville, TN 37203

Association of men and women involved in book publishing and librarians, authors, booksellers, and editors.

THE WRITER
The Writer, Inc.
8 Arlington Street
Boston, MA 02116

Monthly magazine for writers, with articles such as the market for trade journal articles, where to sell manuscripts, quotes for writers, and information about writing opportunities.

WRITER'S DIGEST
205 West Center Street
Marion, OH 43305

Monthly magazine that provides advice on writing, describes trends, indicates needs of publishers, and lists various opportunities. Writer's Digest also publishes *The Business of Being a Writer, How to Be a Successful Housewife/Writer, Travel Writers Handbook, Jobs for Writers, How You Can Make $20,000 a Year Writing, How to Be Happily Published,* and *A Writer's Guide to Book Publishing.* Write to Writer's Digest Books, 9933 Alliance Road, Cincinnati, OH 45242.

WRITERS GUILD OF AMERICA, EAST
22 West 48th Street
New York, NY 10036

Provides a manuscript registration service to prove ownership of a script or work.

WRITERS GUILD OF AMERICA, WEST
8955 Beverly Boulevard
Los Angeles, CA 90048

Publishes a *Newsletter* reporting information regarding jobs and containing a "TV Market List" of television series open to submissions.

WRITER'S HANDBOOK
Edited by Sylvia K. Burack
The Writer, Inc.
8 Arlington Street
Boston, MA 02116

Contains 2,000 listings of where to sell manuscripts; features articles that give practical advice and instruction on writing techniques, agents, and editors; and has chapters by best-selling writers such as John Jakes, Judith Krantz, Isaac Asimov, and Neil Simon.

WRITER'S MARKET
Writer's Digest Books
9933 Alliance Road
Cincinnati, OH 45242

Book published annually and used by professional and creative writers. It lists publishers and types of material they publish; consumer publications; trade, technical, and professional journals; greeting card publishers; author's agents, and contests and awards.

YOU CAN WRITE A PLAY
Milton Polsky
The Rosen Publishing Group
29 East 21st Street
New York, NY 10010

The necessary insight and understanding is given to accomplish this feat.

YOUR FUTURE IN PUBLISHING
Leonard Corwen
Richards Rosen Press
29 East 21st Street
New York, NY 10010

Publishing encompasses many skills from editing to management and writing.

YOUR FUTURE AS A WRITER
Rick Mitz
Richards Rosen Press
29 East 21st Street
New York, NY 10010

First you write to learn, but the background and education necessary is given clearly.

EDUCATION

AMERICAN SOCIETY FOR TRAINING AND DEVELOPMENT
600 Maryland Avenue SW
Washington, DC 20025

Educational association of persons involved in the training and development of personnel in business, education, and government. It provides institutes for training professionals, a member inquiry service, an Operation Talent Match, and a Position Referral Service.

ASSOCIATION FOR COMMUNICATION ADMINISTRATION
5105 Backlick Road, #E
Annandale, VA 22003

Organization of administrators of communication schools, colleges, programs, and departments and administrators of humanities, theater, and English. It focuses on the relationship between academic programs and higher education administration on such matters as management, curriculum, and scholarships. It provides placement services, publishes *Communication Careers*, and has a committee on careers.

ASSOCIATION FOR EDUCATIONAL COMMUNICATIONS AND TECHNOLOGY
1201 Sixteenth Street NW
Washington, DC 20036

Nonprofit organization of persons interested in the uses of media and technology to improve instruction. The AECT has developed competency-based certification guidelines for media personnel. It publishes *Audiovisual Instruction* and *AV Communications Review*. The AECT Placement Service is a clearinghouse for positions such as senior television engineer, audiovisual technician, media specialist, director, instructional communications center, library/media specialist.

ASSOCIATION OF AUDIO-VISUAL TECHNICIANS
P.O. Box 9716
Denver, CO 80209

Association of persons who repair audiovisual systems, train audiovisual technicians, and produce audiovisual materials. Technical information is published, and service seminars are held.

CAREER RESOURCE INFORMATION
American Speech-Language-Hearing Association
10801 Rockville Pike
Rockville, MD 20852

Career information fact sheet on college and university programs in speech pathology and audiology, student financial aid, clinical certification requirements, and graduate education information.

CAREERS IN COMMUNICATION
Association for Communication Administration
5105 Backlick Road #E
Annandale, VA 22003

Published by the ACA, an affiliate of the Speech Communication Association. It examines communications careers from the perspective of communications studies on advertising, communications, film, interpretation, journalism, public relations, radio, speech communication, television, and theater arts. It includes sections on communications competency, employment, the type of careers that communications graduates enter, and brief definitions of each of the communication fields.

CAREERS IN COMMUNICATIONS
Association for Communication Administration
5105 Backlick Road #E
Annandale, VA 22003

Series of eight audio cassettes of a conference on "Careers in Communication" held in July, 1980. The conference was cosponsored by the Association for Communication Administration, the Industrial Communication Council, and the Speech Communication Association.

COMMUNICATION ASSOCIATION OF THE PACIFIC
516 Ulumu Street
Kailua, HA 96734

Educational organization of teachers and students of communications in the context of oral, written, and electronic communication and in radio, television, and film.

COMMUNICATION EDUCATION FOR CAREERS
James H. McBath and David T. Burhans Jr.
ERIC Clearinghouse on Reading and Communication Skills
Speech Communication Association
Annandale, VA 22003

An ERIC/RCS monograph that assesses career potentials of communications education, identifies factors that inhibit and promote such education, and suggests strategies for career planning in the field of speech.

COUNCIL OF COMMUNICATION SOCIETIES
P.O. Box 1074
Silver Springs, MD 20910

Organization of professional societies in communication. It encourages research and educational programs in communication, provides information about communication organizations, and publishes *Guide to Communication Careers.*

EDUCATIONAL COMMUNICATION ASSOCIATION
4000 Massachusetts Avenue NW
Washington, DC 20016

Organization focused on developing and promoting multimedia educational programs. It distributes television and radio programs and maintains a multimedia library.

FOUNDATION FOR PUBLIC RELATIONS RESEARCH AND EDUCATION
415 Lexington Avenue
New York, NY 10017

Association that sponsors and conducts research in public relations. It offers fellowships to university teachers of public relations as well as undergraduate and graduate scholarships to students. It publishes *Public Relations: A Comprehensive Bibliography*, *Public Relations Review*, and *Managing Your Public Relations*.

YOUR FUTURE USING FOREIGN LANGUAGES
E. W. Edwards
Richards Rosen Press
29 East 21st Street
New York, NY 10010

Translating, interpreting, international business all require foreign language skills. How to develop and use these skills are given.

GUIDE FOR JOB CANDIDATES AND DEPARTMENT CHAIRMEN IN ENGLISH AND FOREIGN LANGUAGES
MLA Job Information Service
62 Fifth Avenue
New York, NY 10011

Overview of the job market in higher education in English, writing, and foreign languages. It provides advice on procedures for applying for a position, employment information in junior and community colleges, and how to apply for nonacademic employment.

GRAPHIC ARTS TECHNICAL FOUNDATION
4615 Forbes Avenue
Pittsburgh, PA 15213

Association that does research in graphic processes, conducts educational programs on such subjects as graphic arts textbooks and audiovisuals, and provides a national career and manpower recruitment program. It also provides counseling, aptitude testing, fellowships, and scholarships.

INTERNATIONAL COMMUNICATION ASSOCIATION
Balcones Research Center
10100 Burnet Road
Austin, TX 78758

Educational association of teachers and people from busines, public relations firms, government, and religious organizations. Members study communications in the context of health, information systems, instruction, intercultural situations, interpersonal communication, mass media, organizations, and politics, The association posts classified advertisements for teaching positions in its newsletter. It publishes *Human Communication Research, Journal of Communication*, and *Communication Yearbook*.

INTERNATIONAL TELEVISION ASSOCIATION
136 Sherman Avenue
Berkeley Heights, NJ 07922

Association of persons interested in nonbroadcast television as used in business training and corporate communications. Communications jobs in this field include scriptwriting, producing, consulting, videotape production, and communications needs analysis.

JOB INFORMATION LISTS
MLA Job Information Service
62 Fifth Avenue
New York, NY 10011

List published quarterly to provide the teaching profession in English literature, writing, and foreign languages, with information about job prospects in institutions of higher education.

*THE LAST WORD: EXPLORING CAREERS IN
CONTEMPORARY COMMUNICATIONS*
Members of the Fashion Group
Richards Rosen Press
29 East 21st Street
New York, NY 10010

An Ad Agency Creative Director, Fashion Editor, Public Relations, D.J. Radio Commentator, Filmmaker among others tell about their fields.

MEDIA & METHODS
401 North Broad Street
Philadelphia, PA 19108

Periodical that advertises jobs in the instructional media industry.

NATIONAL ASSOCIATION OF BUSINESS AND EDUCATIONAL RADIO
1330 New Hampshire Avenue
Washington, DC 20036

Association of organizations that are licensed to use two-way radio under the business radio service regulations of the FCC. It publishes statistics on business radio users.

NATIONAL AUDIO-VISUAL ASSOCIATION
3150 Spring Street
Fairfax, VA 22031

Video, audiovisual, and microcomputer products manufacturers, dealers, producers and suppliers are members. Audio Visual America, a seminar and exhibit program, is held annually.

NATIONAL SCHOOL PUBLIC RELATIONS ASSOCIATION
1801 North Moore Street
Arlington, VA 22209

Organization of persons involved in public school public relations. It publishes books, reports, public relations aids, and handbooks.

NATIONAL THEATRE OF THE DEAF
305 Great Neck Road
Waterford, CT 06385

Professional touring group, partly funded by the government, that performs for the handicapped, the deaf, and the general public. It operates the NTD Professional School for Deaf Theatre Personnel, which trains talent to work with public schools and deaf groups. It also provides a service that assists deaf actors in finding employment.

NEW ENGLAND THEATRE CONFERENCE
50 Exchange Street
Waltham, MA 02154

Organization of persons involved in community, educational, and professional theater in New England. It provides a festival for community theater groups, auditions for summer theater jobs, courses on technical theater, and a Theatrical Talent Registry. It publishes *Directory of New England Theatre-Producing Groups*, *Calendar of New England Theatre Events and Productions*, and *Design and Technology*. It also provides a placement bureau.

SOCIETY FOR ADVANCEMENT OF MANAGEMENT
135 West 50th Street
New York, NY 10020

Division of the American Management Associations, it sponsors college and university chapters and is a career starting point for management careers including collective bargaining, quality control, training, marketing, industrial relations, and entrepreneurship.

SOUTHERN SPEECH COMMUNICATION ASSOCIATION
University of West Florida
Pensacola, FL 32504

Organization that promotes the study, understanding, and uses of speech communication. It focuses primarily on communication theory, forensics, intercultural communication, mass media, oral interpretation, rhetoric and public address, speech education, speech and hearing science, and theater. It is affiliated with the Speech Communication Association and provides a placement service.

SPEECH COMMUNICATION ASSOCIATION
5105 Backlick Road, #E
Annandale, VA 22003

Organization of college and public school teachers and speech clinicians. It promotes the study, research, and teaching of law, ethics, government, discussion, debate, learning resources, interpersonal and small group interaction, interpretation, mass communication, public address, rhetorical and communication theory, speech and language sciences, and theater. It maintains a placement service and posts positions in its newsletter, *Spectra*. It also publishes *Communication Education*, *Communication Monographs*, and *Quarterly Journal of Speech*.

Selected List of Colleges with Communications Courses or Majors

Abilene Christian College, Abilene, Texas
Adams State College, Alamosa, Colorado
Adelphi University, Garden City, New York
Akron, University of, Akron, Ohio
Alabama, University of, University, Alabama
Alaska, University of, Fairbanks, Alaska
Allegheny College, Meadville, Pennsylvania
Alma College, Alma, Michigan
American University, Washington, D.C.
Angelo State University, San Angelo, Texas
Appalachian State University, Boone, North Carolina
Arizona State University, Tempe, Arizona
Arizona, University of, Tucson, Arizona
Arkansas State University, Beebe, Arkansas
Arkansas, University of, Fayetteville, Arkansas
Art Institute of Chicago, Chicago, Illinois
Auburn University, Auburn, Alabama
Ball State University, Muncie, Indiana
Baylor University, Baylor, Texas
Bemidji State College, Bemidji, Minnesota
Berry College, Mt. Berry, Georgia
Bloomsburg State College, Bloomsburg, Pennsylvania
Bob Jones University, Greenville, South Carolina
Boise State College, Boise, Idaho
Boston College, Chestnut Hill, Massachusetts
Boston University, Boston, Massachusetts
Bowling Green State University, Bowling Green, Ohio

Bradley University, Peoria, Illinois
Bridgeport, University of, Bridgeport, Connecticut
Bridgewater State College, Bridgewater, Massachusetts
Brigham Young University, Provo, Utah
Brooklyn College, Brooklyn, New York
Broward Community College, Ft. Lauderdale, Florida
Butler University, Indianapolis, Indiana
California State Polytechnic, Pomona, California
California State Polytechnic, San Luis Obispo, California
California State University, Arcata, California
California State University, Chico, California
California State University, Fresno, California
California State University, Fullerton, California
California State University, Hayward, California
California State University, Long Beach, California
California State University, Los Angeles, California
California State University, Northridge, California
California State University, Sacramento, California
California State University, San Diego, California
California State University, San Francisco, California
California State University, San Jose, California
California, University of, Berkeley, California
California, University of, Davis, California
California, University of, Los Angeles, California
California, University of, Santa Barbara, California
Calvin College, Grand Rapids, Michigan
Carnegie-Mellon University, Pittsburgh, Pennsylvania
Case Western Reserve University, Cleveland, Ohio
Catholic University of America, Washington, D.C.
Central Michigan University, Mt. Pleasant, Michigan
Central Missouri State College, Warrensburg, Missouri
Central State University, Edmond, Oklahoma
Central Washington State College, Ellensburg, Washington
Cincinnati, University of, Cincinnati, Ohio
City College, New York, New York
Clarion State College, Clarion, Pennsylvania
Cleveland State University, Cleveland, Ohio
Coe College, Cedar Rapids, Iowa
Colorado State University, Fort Collins, Colorado
Colorado, University of, Boulder, Colorado
Columbia University, New York, New York
Columbus University, Columbus, Ohio

Connecticut, University of, Storrs, Connecticut
Cornell University, Ithaca, New York
C. W. Post College, Greenvale, New York
Dartmouth College, Hanover, New Hampshire
Dayton, University of, Dayton, Ohio
Delaware, University of, Newark, Delaware
Denison University, Granville, Ohio
Denver, University of, Denver, Colorado
DePauw University, Greencastle, Indiana
Detroit, University of, Detroit, Michigan
Drake University, Des Moines, Iowa
Duquesne University, Pittsburgh, Pennsylvania
East Carolina University, Greenville, North Carolina
East Stroudsburg State College, East Stroudsburg, Pennsylvania
East Tennessee State University, Johnson City, Tennessee
East Texas State University, Commerce, Texas
Eastern Illinois University, Charleston, Illinois
Eastern Michigan University, Ypsilanti, Michigan
Eastern New Mexico University, Portales, New Mexico
Eastern Washington State College, Cheney, Washington
Elizabethtown College, Elizabethtown, Pennsylvania
Emerson College, Boston, Massachusetts
Emporia, College of, Emporia, Kansas
Evansville, University of, Evansville, Indiana
Fairfield University, Fairfield, Connecticut
Federal City College, Washington, D.C.
Fisk University, Nashville, Tennessee
Florida State University, Tallahassee, Florida
Florida Technological University, Orlando, Florida
Florida, University of, Gainesville, Florida
Fort Hays Kansas State College, Hays, Kansas
Frostburg State College, Frostburg, Maryland
Gallaudet College, Washington, D.C.
Gannon College, Erie, Pennsylvania
Genessee Community College, Flint, Michigan
Geneva College, Beaver Falls, Pennsylvania
George Washington University, Washington, D.C.
Georgetown College, Georgetown, Kentucky
Georgia, University of, Athens, Georgia
Gonzaga University, Spokane, Washington
Goucher College, Towson, Maryland
Grayson County College, Denison, Texas

Grove City College, Grove City, Pennsylvania
Hartford, University of, West Hartford, Connecticut
Hawaii, University of, Honolulu, Hawaii
Herbert H. Lehman College, Bronx, New York
Hofstra University, Hempstead, New York
Houston, University of, Houston, Texas
Howard University, Washington, D.C.
Humboldt State University, Arcata, California
Hunter College, New York, New York
Idaho State University, Pocatello, Idaho
Idaho, University of, Moscow, Idaho
Illinois State University, Normal, Illinois
Illinois, University of, Chicago, Illinois
Illinois, University of, Urbana, Illinois
Indiana State University, Terre Haute, Indiana
Indiana University, Bloomington, Indiana
Iowa State University, Ames, Iowa
Iowa, University of, Iowa City, Iowa
Ithaca College, Ithaca, New York
Kansas State College, Pittsburg, Kansas
Kansas State Teachers College, Emporia, Kansas
Kansas State University, Manhattan, Kansas
Kansas, University of, Lawrence, Kansas
Kearney State College, Kearney, Nebraska
Kent State University, Kent, Ohio
Kentucky, University of, Lexington, Kentucky
Kingsboro Community College, Brooklyn, New York
Kutztown State College, Kutztown, Pennsylvania
Lamar University, Beaumont, Texas
Lehigh University, Bethlehem, Pennsylvania
Lindenwood College, St. Charles, Mississippi
Linfield College, McMinnville, Oregon
Lock Haven State College, Lock Haven, Pennsylvania
Loma Linda University, Loma Linda, California
Long Island University, Brooklyn, New York
Los Angeles City College, Los Angeles, California
Louisiana Polytechnic Institute, Ruston, Louisiana
Louisiana State University, Baton Rouge, Louisiana
Louisiana State University, New Orleans, Louisiana
Loyola College of Montreal, Montreal, Quebec
Loyola University of California, Los Angeles, California
Macalester College, St. Paul, Minnesota

Madison College, Harrisonburg, Virginia
Maine, University of, Gorham, Maine
Maine, University of, Orono, Maine
Mankato State College, Mankato, Minnesota
Mansfield State College, Mansfield, Pennsylvania
Marietta College, Marietta, Ohio
Marquette University, Milwaukee, Wisconsin
Marshall University, Huntington, West Virginia
Maryland, University of, College Park, Maryland
Marywood College, Scranton, Pennsylvania
Massachusetts, University of, Amherst, Massachusetts
McGill University, Montreal, Quebec
Memphis State University, Memphis, Tennessee
Miami-Dade Junior College, Miami, Florida
Miami, University of, Coral Gables, Florida
Miami University, Oxford, Ohio
Michigan State University, East Lansing, Michigan
Michigan, University of, Ann Arbor, Michigan
Middle Tennessee State University, Murfreesboro, Tennessee
Mills College, Oakland, California
Minnesota, University of, Duluth, Minnesota
Minnesota, University of, Minneapolis, Minnesota
Minnesota, University of, St. Paul, Minnesota
Mississippi State College for Women, Columbus, Mississippi
Mississippi, University of, University, Mississippi
Missouri, University of, Columbia, Missouri
Missouri, University of, Kansas City, Missouri
Montana State University, Bozeman, Montana
Montana, University of, Missoula, Montana
Montclair State College, Upper Montclair, New Jersey
Montevallo, University of, Montevallo, Alabama
Moorhead State College, Moorhead, Minnesota
Morgan State College, Baltimore, Maryland
Mount Union College, Alliance, Ohio
Murray State University, Murray, Kentucky
Nebraska State College, Kearney, Nebraska
Nebraska, University of, Lincoln, Nebraska
Nebraska, University of, Omaha, Nebraska
Nevada, University of, Reno, Nevada
New Hampshire, University of, Durham, New Hampshire
New Mexico State University, Las Cruces, New Mexico
New Mexico State University, University, New Mexico

New Mexico, University of, Albuquerque, New Mexico
New York University, Washington Square, New York, New York
North Adams State College, North Adams, Massachusetts
North Carolina State University, Raleigh, North Carolina
North Carolina, University of, Chapel Hill, North Carolina
North Carolina, University of, Greensboro, North Carolina
North Central Michigan College, Petoskey, Michigan
North Dakota State University, Fargo, North Dakota
North Dakota, University of, Grand Forks, North Dakota
North Texas State University, Denton, Texas
Northeast Louisiana University, Monroe, Louisiana
Northeast Missouri State College, Kirksville, Missouri
Northeast Missouri State College, Maryville, Missouri
Northeastern Illinois University, Chicago, Illinois
Northeastern University, Boston, Massachusetts
Northern Arizona University, Flagstaff, Arizona
Northern Colorado, University of, Greeley, Colorado
Northern Illinois University, DeKalb, Illinois
Northern Iowa, University of, Cedar Falls, Iowa
Northern Michigan University, Marquette, Michigan
Northwestern State College, Alva, Oklahoma
Northwestern State University, Natchitoches, Louisiana
Northwestern University, Evanston, Illinois
Notre Dame, University of, Notre Dame, Indiana
Oberlin College, Oberlin, Ohio
Occidental College, Los Angeles, California
Ohio State University, Columbus, Ohio
Ohio University, Athens, Ohio
Ohio Wesleyan University, Delaware, Ohio
Oklahoma State University, Stillwater, Oklahoma
Oklahoma, University of, Norman, Oklahoma
Orange County Community College, Middletown, New York
Oregon, University of, Eugene, Oregon
Our Lady of the Lake College, San Antonio, Texas
Pace College, New York, New York
Pacific Lutheran University, Tacoma, Washington
Pacific University, Forest Grove, Oregon
Pacific, University of the, Stockton, California
Pembroke State University, Pembroke, North Carolina
Pennsylvania State University, University Park, Pennsylvania
Pepperdine University, Los Angeles, California
Pittsburgh, University of, Pittsburgh, Pennsylvania

Portland State University, Portland, Oregon
Purdue University, Lafayette, Indiana
Queens College, Flushing, New York
Redlands, University of, Redlands, California
Rhode Island College, Providence, Rhode Island
Rhode Island, University of, Kingston, Rhode Island
Richmond, University of, Richmond, Virginia
Rider College, Trenton, New Jersey
Riverside City College, Riverside, California
Rutgers University, New Brunswick, New Jersey
Saint Anselm's College, Manchester, New Hampshire
Saint Cloud State College, St. Cloud, Minnesota
Saint Louis University, St. Louis, Missouri
Saint Mary's College, Winona, Minnesota
Saint Vincent College, Latrobe, Pennsylvania
Samford University, Birmingham, Alabama
San Diego State University, San Diego, California
San Francisco State University, San Francisco, California
San Jose State University, San Jose, California
Seton Hall University, South Orange, New Jersey
Shippensburg State College, Shippensburg, Pennsylvania
Simmons College, Boston, Massachusetts
Skidmore College, Saratoga Springs, New York
Slippery Rock State College, Slippery Rock, Pennsylvania
Smith College, Northampton, Massachusetts
South Dakota State University, Brookings, South Dakota
South Dakota, University of, Vermillion, South Dakota
South Florida, University of, Tampa, Florida
Southeast Missouri State College, Cape Girardeau, Missouri
Southern California, University of, Los Angeles, California
Southern Connecticut State College, New Haven, Connecticut
Southern Illinois University, Carbondale, Illinois
Southern Illinois University, Edwardsville, Illinois
Southern Methodist University, Dallas, Texas
Southern Mississippi, University of, Hattiesburg, Mississippi
Southwest Missouri State College, Springfield, Missouri
Southwest Texas State University, San Marcos, Texas
Stanford University, Stanford, California
Stanislaus State College, Turlock, California
State University of New York, Albany, New York
State University of New York, Buffalo, New York
State University of New York College, Brockport, New York

State University of New York College, Cortland, New York
State University of New York College, Fredonia, New York
State University of New York College, Geneseo, New York
State University of New York College, New Paltz, New York
State University of New York College, Oneonta, New York
State University of New York College, Oswego, New York
State University of New York College, Potsdam, New York
Stephen F. Austin State University, Nacogdoches, Texas
Suffolk University, Boston, Massachusetts
Sul Ross State University, Alpine, Texas
Susquehanna University, Selinsgrove, Pennsylvania
Syracuse University, Syracuse, New York
Temple University, Philadelphia, Pennsylvania
Tennessee, University of, Knoxville, Tennessee
Texas Arts and Industries University, Kingsville, Texas
Texas Christian University, Fort Worth, Texas
Texas Lutheran College, Seguin, Texas
Texas Tech University, Lubbock, Texas
Texas, University of, Arlington, Texas
Texas, University of, Austin, Texas
Texas, University of, El Paso, Texas
Texas Woman's University, Denton, Texas
Toledo, University of, Toledo, Ohio
Toronto, University of, Toronto, Ontario
Towson State College, Baltimore, Maryland
Trenton State College, Trenton, New Jersey
Trinity University, San Antonio, Texas
Tufts University, Medford, Massachusetts
Tulane University, New Orleans, Louisiana
Tulsa, University of, Tulsa, Oklahoma
Utah State University, Logan, Utah
Utah, University of, Salt Lake City, Utah
Vanderbilt University, Nashville, Tennessee
Vermont, University of, Burlington, Vermont
Villanova University, Villanova, Pennsylvania
Virginia Commonwealth University, Charlottesville, Virginia
Wake Forest University, Winston-Salem, North Carolina
Washington State University, Pullman, Washington
Washington, University of, Seattle, Washington
Washington University, St. Louis, Missouri
Wayne State University, Detroit, Michigan
West Chester State College, West Chester, Pennsylvania
West Florida University, Pensacola, Florida

West Texas State University, Canyon, Texas
West Virginia University, Morgantown, West Virginia
Western Carolina University, Collowhee, North Carolina
Western Illinois University, Macomb, Illinois
Western Kentucky University, Bowling Green, Kentucky
Western Michigan University, Kalamazoo, Michigan
Western State College of Colorado, Gunnison, Colorado
Western Washington State College, Bellingham, Washington
Whittier College, Whittier, California
Wichita State University, Wichita, Kansas
William Paterson College, Wayne, New Jersey
Winona State College, Winona, Minnesota
Wisconsin, University of, Eau Claire, Wisconsin
Wisconsin, University of, La Crosse, Wisconsin
Wisconsin, University of, Madison, Wisconsin
Wisconsin, University of, Milwaukee, Wisconsin
Wisconsin, University of, Oshkosh, Wisconsin
Wisconsin, University of, Platteville, Wisconsin
Wisconsin, University of, River Falls, Wisconsin
Wisconsin, University of, Stevens Point, Wisconsin
Wisconsin, University of, Superior, Wisconsin
Wisconsin, University of, Whitewater, Wisconsin
Wyoming, University of, Laramie, Wyoming